Aspects of Art

Aspects of Art

Justin Schorr

South Brunswick · New York:
A. S. Barnes and Company
London: Thomas Yoseloff Ltd

A. S. Barnes and Co., Inc.
Cranbury, New Jersey 08512

Thomas Yoseloff Ltd
18 Charing Cross Rd.
London W. C. 2, England

6534
Printed in the United States of America

Acknowledgments

AS AUTHOR MY GREATEST DEBT IS TO THOSE WRITERS, SOME cited in the bibliography, some regrettably forgotten, who have stimulated the thinking displayed herein. For great aid and continuing encouragement, I am indebted to Professor Edwin Ziegfeld of Teachers College, Columbia University.

The debt I owe as a person and a painter to my parents and my wife is incalculably great; to them I dedicate this book.

Introduction

THE ART STUDENT NOW HAS ADDRESSED TO HIM, IN BOOKS
and in the schools, much instruction on how to paint. And
pursuant to such instruction the neophyte spends most of
his time before the easel, learning, as every artist must,
the ways and means of his art. However, he soon finds
that his books and teachers, while fostering indispensable
skills, do not speak to many of his most serious questions.
For the student wants not only to be artistically compe-
tent but also to see his life in art as making some sort of
sense. He wants grounds for believing that his work re-
lates to himself, the art world, and the community at large
in a choate, worthwhile way. If such belief is precluded
then learning how-to-do-it seems meaningless, absurd. Yet
no one speaks to him about *being an artist*, only about art
practice; his questions are ignored.

Furthermore, his concerns are often of urgent, immediate, practical interest; they cannot be put off as being of a
purely theoretic nature or of no immediate consequence,
and so one wonders why little attention is given to these
problems. For example, through reading art publications

and visiting galleries and museums the student gathers that under the heading "art objects" can be listed tightly-designed, crystal-like organizations of objects, colors, and forms *and* (apparently) disjointed agglomerations. Also, vitally important seems deft and sensitive handling of materials *and* (apparently) brutish execution. Sometimes the most profound ideas and feelings seem central to art, but often seemingly contentless paintings are equally esteemed. Heretofore, in times of little artistic diversity students drew the comforting (if unsound) inference that "art object" meant "a thing like that which is currently held to be such by artists, museum people and patrons"; but the variety we face precludes such inference drawing (see Plates 1, 2, 3), and we have no grounds for decreasing this variety; to do so would be merely arbitrary and it would impoverish art. So, on the face of things, art seems to be anything-at-all, and if it *is* so in fact, then art and its makers are nothing in particular, of no especial function or worth in the world. Hence, dependent upon his finding a satisfactory response to the question, "What characterizes the art object?" is the artist's identity and morale. On this matter, we see, theory and behavior are closely linked.

Also, the student's choices as to with *whom* and exactly *what* he will study, and eventually his choice of stylistic direction, hinge largely upon his responses to theoretic questions. And rendering such responses is difficult. For example, most serious thinkers agree that no one artistic path is theoretically privileged over others, yet as the student considers teachers and curricula he finds that each traditionalist has a *particular* tradition that he conveys to his students, while each revolutionary trains men for *his* revolutionary army (or makes revolution itself mandatory, thus academic and a bore). In practice, privi-

1. Willem de Kooning, *Composition* (1955). In the face of art's diversity, do we search for a common denominator, or say art is nothing in particular, or—what? (See also Plates 2 and 3.) (Solomon R. Guggenheim Museum)

2. Vermeer, *Young Woman with Water Jug*. (See Plate 1.) (The Metropolitan Museum of Art, Gift of Henry G. Marquand, 1889)

3. Robert Rauschenberg, *First Landing Jump* (1961). (See Plate 1.)
(Collection of Philip C. Johnson, promised gift to the Museum of
Modern Art, New York. Photographed by Eric Pollitzer)

lege is being claimed—and unconvincingly. One cannot try to learn *all* skills, but on what basis can the student decide what to study? And how does the developing artist find a direction for his work? These are theoretic questions, but also very practical ones, to which few men speak.

Also, while artists do not need to comprehend creative behavior in order to be creators, they must know enough, for example, to nurture their talents and heed those impulses of good artistic potential. Yet students are sometimes so enmeshed in questions on creative conduct that they cannot judge the potential of an idea, or decide when pre-planning and when improvisation is proper painterly conduct for them. Again, questions on creative process are theoretic *while* practical.

Being a student, someone under instruction, itself raises questions, of consequence to both learner and teacher. What sorts of development can be fostered in schools—art skills? personal maturation?—and who is responsible for fostering such development? How may student and teacher stand with respect to each other, so that ideas and insights can be transmitted without breeding dependence? Theory and practice are inseparable in these questions also.

Now it seems natural that how-to-do-it books and courses would not speak to these questions; but then too, though the student may expect otherwise, books in art philosophy and psychology also do not help much with the artist's queries. And upon reflection this also is quite understandable. It is not, and cannot be, the practice of art theorists to pick their questions chiefly with regard to what painters need to know, and to press their inquiries only to the extent of the artist's interest. It is the philosopher's interests and audience that must be served. Hence, although *some* of the above questions cannot be, and are not, ignored by reflective writers, others are, while some issues of no interest to artists are explored at great length. In sum, philosophers do not speak directly to or for artists; and while art students sometimes read philosophy to their benefit, the price for such benefit in terms of time and effort is high.

Further complicating the neophyte's problem is the fact that while little is addressed directly to his questions, much quasi-theoretical material is given to him inadvertently by teachers and colleagues, in the form of the language they speak, the ideas they bandy about, the intellectual climate they create. Also, much of this material consists of untested and untrustworthy assumptions, empty or erroneous platitudes, and fuzzily stated hunches. And while an artist can·do very well without *any* good philosophy he cannot do so well holding firmly to a bad position. When his notions fight with his experience, when his actual perceptions find no place in his scheme of things, he is in a bind—or just confused. Yet with the theoretic material generally imbibed by students, conflicts and confusion are almost unavoidable. Students pick up the notion that a painting is "a statement," that it ought to "say something." And they hear that "every form has its expressive face." But then they are troubled by paintings which are undeniably impressive but which do not so much say anything as they apparently perform visual marvels, or which are not so much statements as they are silent good company. And while a form may have an expressive face, this aspect of the form may be less important than its numinous or magic-making qualities. But can the student make his forms less expressive but more awesome (consider the pyramid) when expression theory haunts our classrooms and studios, and when forms which do not state are regarded as nothing? Philosophers have long questioned the general adequacy of expression theory and have shaken some of its particular claims, yet it seems safe to guess that for every one hundred artists, teachers, and students who talk "expression" there is only one who has read critiques of expression theory and has considered amplifications of or alternatives to it. It is no wonder, then, that the student has difficulty making sense of things, for either no one speaks to his questions or he does so unclearly and inadequately.

Where, then, can the student go with his questions? I submit that while everyone who teaches and studies art recognizes the need for instruction in the craft and history of painting, for practice in the art, and for literature to support this instruction, little recognition is given to the need for consideration of such problems as cited above and for literature to aid with such consideration. Yet the need exists. The following essays are intended as a beginning to the literature that will be called for as the need is admitted. They are aimed at helping the student deal with his questions; they give him at least one place to go with his queries.

Let me make clear the sort of help offered, by first saying what is *not* to be found herein. As a painter I do have a personal aesthetic, but it will not appear (except inadvertently) in these pages. Though one might argue that presentation of such an aesthetic could help students by serving as a temporary crutch (or an irritant) or to simply start a dialogue, too often a mere personal turn of mind is identified by author and reader as a great truth—and this is misleading.

Also, the reader should not expect to find, as a polar opposite to a personal aesthetic, a comprehensive systematic art philosophy. Provision of such is beyond my abilities, and would interest few artists and students in any case.

Rather, I confront here some theoretic problems which I had to face as an artist, and some others which I see my students and colleagues facing. This is a personal and quite limited selection, then; but unless my experience is strangely atypical this will be to the good, since, as we noted, a choice of questions on the basis of artists' interests is precisely what the student needs and cannot find.

In response to *some* of the questions, a case is made for a particular position. However, many of the following pages contain only arguments against currently prevalent views. And still other pages present not a substantive claim but a sketch for a way of thinking about a problem, a frame of thought upon which the question can hang deferred, this because artists often need not to have answers but to have the terror removed from the questions.

All of which is to say that these essays offer not a resting place but rather a springboard into discussions of a few of the issues bedeviling the neophyte. Currently such discussions are extra-curricular, occurring in bull sessions and the like, but they are too important to remain dependent upon chance and without intellectual support. I hope these pages will be the beginning of such support.

Contents

Illustrations

Illustrations

I

The Art-Appreciative
Phenomenon and Its Object

WHAT LIES AT THE HEART OF THE ART STUDENT'S CURRENT
questions about art objects?

Consider the artist's classic pattern of behavior in regard to the admissibility as art of the things he and his
colleagues produce. He admits as "a work of art" objects
which "act like art" in the world; when an item performs,
in experience, in a manner he identifies with the realm of
art, he is willing to call the item a citizen of the realm.
And this is why art citizenship requirements change (although slowly sometimes); this is change geared to and in
accordance with demonstrations, in experience, of an ap-
plicant's entry rights. Note which is the driving gear of
this enmeshed pair. One hears, "This painting feels so
right that, despite our current notions and statutes (about
art qualities), it can't be wrong. And should we not then
change our notions to accord with this work's demon-

strated rightness?" The artist's conception of the qualities of the art object, are thusly *kept open and geared to the thrust of performance,* in that he lets an object's capacities in experience tell him imperatively that this item's qualities, whatever they are, *are* art qualities.

Now the reflective person will see several difficulties in this pattern of behavior. One is that the artist, if his openness is not to be mere soft-headedness, needs grounds for believing that he means something in particular when he states that an object "acts like art" in experience, and for believing that the statement points to goings on of a distinctive sort, an art sort. And such grounds are not currently in the artist's grasp.

However, this would not normally disturb the artist; he would remain steady if the behavior pattern described remained otherwise unassailed. But assailed it is. For the artist today often doubts that he can keep his conception of art changing in pace and in accordance with the actual inclusions he makes, pursuant to the pattern cited. And if he cannot, he is in difficulty. Works exhibited as art objects currently display such a diverse and apparently disparate lot of properties and, one surmises, operate to such a multitude of ends, that to admit them all is to make art seem to be merely anything at all—*unless* one's conception of art reasonably embraces the lot and indicates why they *are* all sensibly admissible under one heading, despite their differences. Only with such a conception can the artist's behavior pattern *and* his esteem for art as a profession be maintained. When we see one or the other weakened, as we do, we know such a conception is lacking. And it is this lack, with its threat to a valued pattern of conduct and to the artist's self-respect, that prompts the neophyte to ask theoretic questions about the art object.

What to do, then, in response?

No one addressing himself to artists young or old can seriously suggest abandoning the behavior pattern cited above; that pattern is accepted here. And this is to say that the current and ever-increasing spectrum of (art) qualities is accepted here as a fact of (aesthetic) life. Moreover (to begin the lines of my argument) I think we must take this fact of life as an indication that we will never find grounds for grouping objects under the special heading "art" by attempting to find a least common denominator among the qualities of these objects. Their properties are too disparate.

Is there, then, a distinctive function that art objects fulfill, a function that unifies into one family all things which perform this function, despite the members' great property differences? Many men have tried to point to a particular job that the art object does; many today, including myself, doubt that such pointing can be successful. One gathers that art indeed works in human life but does not do only one distinctive "art" sort of work.

Let us not, then, try to identify and unify art workers by citation of a common uniform or badge, a quality, or property, least common denominator. And for this unification, let us also not seek a particular sort of art function as this denominator.

There is at least one other alternative. We noted that admission is granted to objects which "act like art" in awareness. If we do not inquire as to the ends to which the art object acts, nor to the properties it requires in order to so act, we may, still, inquire into this *way* of acting in awareness, asking, "Is this way a distinctive one?" More precisely, I wish to examine the phenomenon of art appreciative experience and to see whether it is possible, through description of the conditions obtaining in this phenomenon, to display it as a distinctive sort of goings-on in the world, whose conditions in practice and theory are sufficient to make men perceive an instance when such conditions obtain as being one of the aesthetic sort, as distinct from instances of, say, religious phenomena, games, and nature appreciation. If such description is afforded, then our worker, the art object, is identifiable by how he shows up on the work site and by his manner of working: the phenomenology of his appearance.

And, if such description can be rendered, we can sensibly talk of art objects as indeed one family; a family whose members have in common an especial potential for inciting the (described) distinctive aesthetic sort of occurrences. We will surmise beforehand from our acquaintance with art objects that this potential, though a special one, is quite variously constituted. But since family membership rests only upon possession of this potential, the variety of factors constituting it does not make for strained relations.

Also, we can use the findings of our phenomenological examination as clues to what constitutes the art potential in different cases, proceeding much as have others who, for example, discerned (all too simplistically) an "aesthetic emotion" in appreciative experience and took this as a directive to search for emotion-incitive qualities in the object. The properties one may discern through this procedure cannot be exhausted, but even a partial list helps us render a plausible model of how objects can indeed foster the experience described. And this increases the credibility of the presentation.

To the extent that my effort is successful (and debate about a phenomenological examination is inescapable), will it constitute a *definition* of "art objects?" I think so. Although it does seem strange to read words about how objects *appear* and to hear claimed about these words that they *define*. For it seems that to speak about how something *appears* is not to say what it *is;* and to define one must speak of what *is*. However, I am suggesting that we have failed to learn what the art object is (and what a game is) because we have failed to see that what *is*, what really constitutes an art object as such, is *only a capacity to appear* in a certain distinctive way. I am claiming that the art object has not distinctive properties or functions but a distinctive appearance capacity, a phenomenal face identical with no other, and to define this capacity is to define "art object."

Yet more important than whether this effort offers definition or not is the fact that, if they are convincing, the following pages indicate that the artist does point to something real and distinctive when he says an object acts like art in his awareness. And these pages will tell the artist that he can feel warranted in saying that, considering the absence of a quality or function least common denominator, all he *knows* that art objects have in common is their potential for inciting a particular (the aesthetic) sort of goings on; and when an item has this potential, however constituted, he finds no reason to raise barriers to its admission as art and indeed feels justified in admitting the item. The classic pattern of behavior is thusly endorsed without, however, indicating that the admission policy makes of art anything at all.

Let us look, then, at those confrontations of a subject with an object wherein what the subject takes to be aesthetic value, however it is to be described, is apparently realized—experientially apprehended rather than either merely acknowledged as realizable—or seems unrealizable; and wherein, furthermore, this apprehension of value is so prominent as to move the subject to believe that the object is a work of art: an item whose reason for

being includes the profference of such value. Such situations do occur. Let us not try to describe them exhaus-
tively; they have too many levels, shadings, idiosyncrasies,
ambivalences for any rendition to display completely. Let
us not look for what is, or is not, most valued in such experience. Since it is definition we are after, and not com-
pleteness or role in life, let us ask, "What conditions obtain
in the phenomena which mark them as distinctive, and in
all differentiate them from other sorts of situations?"

One condition which marks those occasions when a
man finds an object to be a work of art is that he finds the
object engaging, gripping. In reference to art experience,
men speak of being taken (e.g., "taken by beauty") or
moved, captivated, entranced, employing metaphorical
terms which point beyond mere interest and liking to the
hold on or enmeshment of awareness art objects may
achieve, sometimes brief (Plate 4), sometimes lasting
(Plate 5), always intimate.

Indeed, the art object *by* engaging a subject circum-
scribes and crystallizes "a situation" out of the routine
flow of his environment and experience. If one reflects
upon an experience with a work of art he recalls that the
object demarcates what he sees from all else—adjacent
wall space and the flow of time could just as well not exist
for all it registers in one's mind during appreciation of a
painting—and in so doing the object constitutes, in so far
as the subject's awareness is concerned, "what is at hand."
Art appreciation is thusly hallmarked by its being an individual object–subject conjunction, a situation, with a particular locus in time and space, whether of long or short
duration.

Another hallmark of such aesthetic experience is the
obligatory, the ought-to-be-so, quality of the seeing un-
dergone within it. When a painting is exhibited it seems to

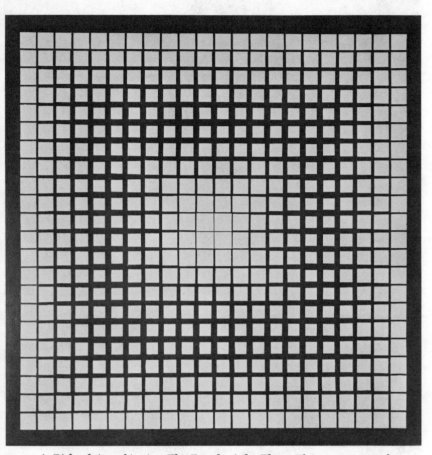

4. Richard Anuszkiewicz, *The Fourth of the Three.* The engagement of viewer and painting can be brief and harsh—but intimate and gripping still. (Collection of Whitney Museum of American Art, New York. Photographed by O. E. Nelson)

5. Rembrandt, *Self Portrait*. The engagement of viewer and painting can be long and tender—and always intimate. (The Frick Collection)

say, as it were, "Attend to me," and the person who finds it to be a work of art does not find himself asking, "Why should I (attend)?" but rather finds on the face of things that this item *should be* attended to.[1]

I do not say that the art object's claim upon attention is an overwhelmingly compelling or even an especially mighty one, but only that the demand looms as obligatory, perhaps alongside others of greater and lesser urgency.

Art-appreciative situations are also hallmarked by a peculiar alignment of the subjectivity of the person participating in it; by his distinctive way of taking the sight afforded by the object. This way is the oft-noted if ill defined "aesthetic attitude." Let us try to specify what characterizes this, the art-taking posture, and what distinguishes it from all others, so that my claim that it characterizes an aesthetic occurrence may have some specific content.

The appreciative attitude is one which is assumed not through deliberation and intention; it is caused rather than reasoned into being; it "comes about." Interior factors may have to be ready for this coming-about and may greatly participate in it, but the stance-taking behavior is an act stimulated from without. And I wish to argue that the stimulus for the assumption of the appreciative taking-posture is the apparency or conspicuousness of the *type* of the given offered for taking. Usually, when something is evidently given as a proposal it elicits an appropriate reception attitude: one of consideration. Something evidently a memory stimulates a reminiscent taking-posture. One becomes exploratory when taking something evidently a supposition. The art object, because its mode of givenness is evident, is also taken in a stance appropriate for this type of given. What type? Let us point to it by using painting as our model art.[2]

Paintings offer sights as images. That is, one is given by a painting not just something one can see but a sight evidently proffered to be *just* seen; that which is proffered as an image, one finds, is not merely visible but looms *as* a vision. It seems to have *being* in order to "just be" in awareness; it seems to be for regard. (And if one senses the psychic alignment entailed in the regard attitude and does not tie the word only to the visual, he may sense what my allegations about the aesthetic attitude are for the arts other than painting.) And it is therefore, because in art appreciation one is taking a sight given as such, that one is taking, appropriately, in a neutral just-let-it-be attitude. In this sense the aesthetic is a dispassionate attitude, as is so often said. Yet it is an affectable man who is "just-being" with the image and hence one who is, possibly, also caring, involved, though involved only as with the object to be regarded.

I urge that this view is the only sensible recourse on this matter, that it seems implausible to believe that the art object is given as other than (in painting) an image, a regard-thing. If say, a tree is depicted in a painting (Plate 6), consider the possibilities: the tree is existant, but clearly is not given to the viewer as a perception. Of course one perceives (via retina, optical nerve, etc.) the rendering of tree but he does not find tree or depiction given *as* a perception, a thing of the world one has "run into." Nor does the tree appear as a memory; it does not loom as a once-known tree recalled. Obviously many depicted things could not be subject to recollection, having never existed to be seen and remembered, but even a still life of familiar objects does not appear as "a sight memory has brought back."

And one must find unconvincing any argument which claims the sight a painting affords is given as a supposi-

6. Vincent Van Gogh, *Cypresses*. The given is a sight or vision, as such; i.e., given as image. (The Metropolitan Museum of Art, Rogers Fund, 1949)

tion, or as an hypothesis, or a delineation of a possibility, or as a pretense; though such may be included in paint.ings, one finds little reason to believe that as such they are given. The modes of sup-position, and hypo-thesis, as well as the possibility, are related to belief and the believability of a given, being modes which are easily entertainable in *this* respect. However, one is not forced into suggesting that an art sight, because it is also easily entertainable, is given in one of these modes—the suggestion which apparently underlies the arguments we are noting—for one does not have to think of art as submitted in the domain of belief and believability at all but rather submitted as a presence to be with, a candidate for company rather than intellection. In other words, the painting-sight *may* be readily entertainable because it is good company and not, necessarily, entertainable because admission into thought is easier for that which is given as, say, a supposition than as a proposition; the alternatives are not only among modes of thought, hence the art and the supposition (or other thought-holding) mode need not be considered identical, as the only recourse for explaining art's admissibility into awareness. And a painting actually does proffer a sight and, often, depictions within it; these *are* presences, they have being. Can one sensibly say that Michelangelo's Jehovah (Plate 20) or Mondrian's rectangles (Plate 23) are givens to be supposed, hypothesized, or for that matter pretended, into being when one views a painting, that is, somehow realized into a being other than that of the image-presence it already is? Surely one does not even tentatively or fancifully or conjecturally find paintings bringing such things into one's awareness except as visions of them given as such; these things do not become thoughts, however held, or presences as others than images (how present?), but in appreciation remain *sights*.

Indeed it cannot even mean anything to talk of a Jackson Pollock abstraction (see Plate 13) as a supposition (what does one have to suppose?) or of behaving "as if" it were real, for in no way could it be more real than it already is, and in no way does it bid one think about anything else as somehow real or to be realized. The sight a painting affords must be given in a mode other than that of the supposition, hypothesis, possibility, or pretense.

Is an art appearance given as a statement, a source of insight, or an embodiment of feeling; that is, as an expression? Of course, many paintings render incarnate and hence display—in this sense they press out into the world —beliefs, insights, feelings, states of mind. In specific cases this incarnation may be the factor that more than any other tends to make the painting loom as gripping. But this is not the case with all paintings nor even with a number sufficient to prompt, by the consistency of paintings' appearances, viewers to find paintings to be that which is given as expressions, as one does find of lectures. (See Plate 7.) It is a sheer fact of life that men find paintings given as items which *somehow* manage to loom as sights to be seen, be it through their sometime expressiveness or loveliness or libidinous appeal or anything else; that is, whatever are the *causes* of the item's demand upon visual attention, they do not proclaim their nature. Hence paintings do not loom as, say, editorials or love-objects, but rather as sights—the only thing they openly purport to be.

So men indicate by their not asking of the assertions embodied in (some) paintings: "Is this true?" Or of paintings expressive of a particular "feel" of life: "Does life indeed feel this way?" And so a man indicates by accepting sentimentalized *and* mordant views of life; naturally one does not consider the truthfulness or aptness or the

7. Max Beckmann, *The Descent from the Cross,* 1917. The painting is expressive, but not given as, and indeed being more than "an expression." (Collection, Museum of Modern Art, New York. Curt Valentin Bequest. Photographed for the Museum by Soichi Sunami)

consistency with one's own viewpoint of that which is not given as an exhibitor of any sort of truth, intellectual, emotional, psychical, or other. Indeed, whatever may be expressed, though operative, is not *considered* at all; the beliefs and feelings displayed in a work of art are experientially tested as presences in awareness, tried out as beings for one's company. Our unspoken question is "What is it like to be in the presence of this sayer saying thus-and-so (whether thus-and-so is good or bad, right or wrong)?" For we expect, when something looms as an image, only that the image's promise be fulfilled, that the item saying, "Regard me" will be well worth regarding, somehow. And the very occurrence of this, and only this, expectation points to the mode of givenness, which prompts the taking-posture; that of the image—the regard-thing.

A painting, then, in looming as an image, seems only an appearance put up in awareness, to be held there for the experience of living with this thing in regard for a while. In so looming it calls not for one's affirmation or denial, either in thought processes or behavior. One *may* respond to the image—he is an operative human being holding this item in regard—but one does not stand as though called upon to respond. In standing uncalled-upon for response the person's mind-set is different even from that entailed in remembering, for one necessarily gets "tight" and self-interested with a memory; a recalled real-life event often brings renewed serious consideration ("Did I do right or wrong?") and even a re-view of a pleasurable scene which one wants to loll around with in memory may have guilt or fear associated with it. Also, supposing, positing, hypothesizing, fantasizing, call for the stances of exploration, consideration, testing, and moving (perhaps tentatively) into new positions; call for a coping and going-out of the person, which art appreciation may include incidentally but does not entail. The image just seems here to be looked at, to *just be* in awareness; and one lets-it-be, one is neutral toward it. In this sense one is dispassionate in art situations. When a sight is given to behold, one, in letting *it* be also lets *oneself* just be. So we say not that in this neutral "just being" stance one need never think, or that one's needs and personality cease to function, that one is indifferent or is actually nullified as a person when seeing a work of art; but that whatever one is just operates, that one is conjoined with an object in art situations but is neither looking for something, nor looking after oneself, nor engaged in this or that endeavor. Even ideas, beliefs, and one's own stirred passions loom in this attitude as "givens," regardables; one is neutral in that one accepts the givenness of it all.

As mentioned, it is especially important that this regarding attitude, as a hallmark of appreciative phenomena, be understood by anyone who would extend my line of thought to arts other than painting. For the mode of attention I wish to point to perhaps is clearly indicated for paintings by the term "just seeing," and for music, one would say, the "regarding" appreciator is "just hearing." But within such arts as architecture, appreciation involves experiencing a building by, for example, not only seeing it but walking through it: perceiving the pacing of its turnings, its large vis à vis small spaces, the very feel of its floors, being aware of how its utilitarian functions are fulfilled by the structure, and so on. Such experiencing involves tactile and aural as well as visual perception, and it involves time, memory, knowledge, and cognitions (e.g., of the builder's needs). What makes such experiencing on occasion an art-appreciative rather than just a common usage of the building is that then the undergoing is in art's special mode; one, for example, not only perceptively feels one's body walking as in any other stroll but contemplates one's walking, holds it before one's attention for regard. (How is it to walk here?) Even as one goes to a business appointment in the building, if one is appreciating the building as art one is aware of finding dispassionately how it "feels" to go to such an appointment in this instance. Even the blurred edge between modes of experience—the business and aesthetic, in this instance—is a regardable. One is not psychically distanced in such an experience, but one is taking it in art's distinctive mode of reception, holding it up in awareness. One not only takes the givens but holds their givenness in regard.

Another hallmark of the appreciative situation is that the object in it seems a thing proffered, something presented by a man to a man; a thing handed to one rather than an inadvertency. Usually the work exhibits conspicuous evidence, (for example, in its being more obviously organized or contrived than raw nature) that it is a profference, an offering by a giver responsible for this present. Yet, strangely and intriguingly, the giving act and its outcome seem, from the face of the object, necessary, as though beyond being for the artist's credit or responsibility. The object seems at once called forth (responsibly given) yet so much called-for as to make this particular giving apparently inevitable; it seems a thing done "by design," yet "natural," an apparently uncontrived resultant of forces, which seemingly had to work out this particular way.[3] Indeed, it is this appearance of a painting as a responsibly offered presentation that constitutes a part of the object's power to grasp our attention, for while natural events and objects *may* catch our attention they do not do so with such consistent success as human *bids* for it, as someone or something evidently saying, "Here, take this, harken, see."

One testifies to the point that an object looming as a work of art normally seems responsibly given when he shows disturbance at the absence of such an appearance, at, for example, an exhibition as art of "found objects," or paintings apparently accidental in execution, or copies. Of such objects the exhibitor, it might seem, is not the responsible giver, hence when such is their appearance one cannot take them in the aesthetic mode of reception. Aesthetic reception becomes possible when one realizes that selection among existing things is a way of giving (Plate 11) and so is creating dualisms between art and everyday objects (Plate 3) and between randomness and contrivance (Plate 13), and so is contriving situations wherein certain sorts of "accidents" are likely to occur; that is, when one's taking is made into a response to what he understands to be an art sort of giving through an increase in understanding of what such giving may involve.

And to the art object's normally seeming necessitated we testify when we speak, as men do, of a painting seeming "logical"—though in an indescribable logic; or "purposive"—without a purpose; or "right"—though in no namable respect; or "working"—to no citable end. And the persistence of questions about the fount of artistry (e.g., Is the artist a seeker for, or a tool of, quasi-divine powers?) and the basis of creative necessitation also testifies that art objects do inexplicably seem profferences which have to be as they are; their existence and their appearance seem necessitated.

In sum, I have urged thus far that a painting when looming as a work of art seems a thing necessitated and proffered for one's visual attention and *to be* so taken; one which conscripts the subject's awareness, and it seems rightfully so. Moreover, it seems a thing given for and right for the neutrally contemplative, the regard sort of attention. But now, in the borderland between substantive and phenomenological inquiry, let us approach the question of what characterizes the objects which foster such goings-on. What are their apparent capacities and what qualities constitute such capacities?

As directed by clues drawn from the foregoing description and direct experience of art objects, I would portray each such object as an item which is, first of all, an individual, a "this thing," a being (though not necessarily unique), which seems to have an identity or "personality."[4] And this thing has had, and must have, to loom as it does, a capacity for making its presence realized. It has in theater parlance, "stage presence." In our model art, painting, this individual normally shows up in sight as a visual field which is discrete, bounded, and both varied and unified enough to constitute a system or world to live in. Moreover, somewhat like the human circulatory or reproductive systems, it exists to some avail, it is purposive; it is somehow good or for a good. And in a way I shall specify at length, it is visually marvelous. It would not loom as "to be seen" otherwise. In so being it seems eminently suited to, indeed binding upon, the regard sort of attention; a world *to be* focused upon, lived in, a being to (just) be with.

Let me now try to give content and fullness to this sketch of the art object and to draw the theoretic lines of distinction between this and other sorts of objects; although, because the art object is a dense amalgam of (the cited) qualities coexisting and coincident with each other, it is difficult to portray it by a linear exposition.

Perhaps we can best begin to display what it means for

an item to appear as a realized individual, as a "this thing," by noting that in daily life the content of one's awareness often seems to loom as "a number of things," or as "a part of something," or as "nothing." One sees, for example, a boy, a dog, a house, a car; and sees these perhaps not even as "this scene" but as "a number of things"—miscellaneous, non-cohering environment. (So the items loom, singly and as a batch, although each may be in fact an individual.) Or one may see bricks which singly and in all appear as "a part of a house," or the house and its environs as "a part of things in general," or "a part . . . of the passing scene." (Again, despite the fact that the boy, dog, brick, house, is each a complete thing.)

Or, that which one confronts may despite its substantiality appear as "nothing." So we indicate when we sometimes reply to the questions, "What did you do the last hour?" and, "What did you then see?" by saying, "Nothing." Obviously one sees and does real things each hour, but the noted reply indicates that the reality of one's behavior and of the items one contacted does not assure that these loomed in awareness as realized. And, of course, the not-realized is as nothing in awareness.

Or, one's view may apparently consist of a cohesive integer, with bounds and form; one which, moreover, seems necessary for constituting *this* vision. The visual integer may be This Scene—somehow made, and made a realized presence, out of the ever-present scenery about us—or a person or structure which comprizes a focus for, and field of, attention; a magnet around which attention gathers (Plate 8) or a world in which awareness lives (Plate 9). Then it looms as having a particular identity— seeming to be "in essence, this," or "at heart, that"—even when *what* the thing at heart is, is ineffable. It is in this manner, I am suggesting, the art object looms.

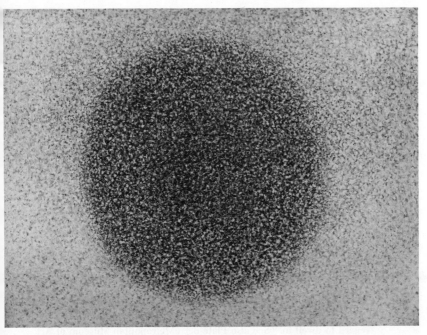

8. Richard Pousette-Dart, *Radiance*, 1962–63. For attention, a magnet to focus it. (See also Plate 9.) (Collection, The Museum of Modern Art, New York. Gift of Susan Morse Hilles. Photographed by Geoffrey Clements.)

9. Rubens, *Wolf and Fox Hunt*. A field (or world) made optimal for regard to dwell in. (See also Plate 8.) (Metropolitan Museum of Art, Kennedy Fund, 1910)

But what is there about the art object which tends to make it so loom? First (undivorceable from its other characteristics) the object's structure gives it a great potential for appearing as a realized field of, or focus for, visual attention. It has a structure that exhibits especial viability for such reception and attention, in that, for one thing, it proffers to vision *directly* that which men ordinarily have to *construct* of the visual world in order to attend to or reside in it insightfully. And naturally such a structure would foster, though not fully account for, the "to be seen" appearance of the art object. As Lincoln Rothschild puts it:

The tremendous mass of stimuli constantly presented to the human senses would give rise to paralysing confusion were it not for the faculty of attention, which makes possible selection of centers for concentration. The function of the artist in an important degree is to present the senses with an experience in which the elements are pre-coordinated so perfectly that attention may grasp the whole, feeling power in a microcosm devoid of elusive irrelevances.[5]

I would buttress this view and state more explicitly what viable structure consists of, and how it functions, by observing that artists have long symptomized their awareness of it. When noting that their paintings seem unified, varied, balanced, harmonious, continuous, etc., they exhibited, in all, what they often termed "the design qualities." Indeed, when teaching, they have often insisted that exhibition of such qualities is minimal for aesthetic admissibility. Such insistence, though faulty in some respects soon to be noted, may be seen as revealing a genuine intuition about the nature of art, and as supportive of the aforementioned views when one sees the "design qualities" as functioning aspects of, hence coincident with, a visually viable structure; and, moreover, sees them as usually entailed in what it means to be a "this thing," an individual, a work of art.

Reflection indicates that an item in object-of-regard status in awareness seems to have bounds—bounds that are its own; apparently "this thing" seems to exist. In being "this thing" it necessarily extends thus far; its bounds seem both to belong to and to be of a oneness with itself. This appearance, we may understand, would conduce to attention; the thing that seems of a piece seems therein graspable in attention, whereas the endless or indeterminate, or a miscellaneous and arbitrarily demarcated slice of stuff, or something larger than, or too fragmentary to be grasped as, an Individual or "this thing," would not conduce to attention; one would not know "what to make of it." And this is to say that something looming as object-of-regard appears as a *unity*, being neither more, less, nor other than a one-thing. And the unity of an item fosters, to some extent at least, object-of-regard status for it.

But a unity or integer in order to best stand out from "things in general" and not be an unrealized "member of the crowd" must be conspicuously distinctive, "a real individual," a marked identity; any integer which seems just so much more of the same stuff always around us does not especially call for attention. And requisite for, indeed synonymous with, these qualities are those of *dominance* and *variety*. The particular variety exhibited by a work demarcates it from the routine, the continuous, the stuff that goes on and on and on, which is boring, lacking distinction, and hence not inviting to attention. And variety acts in awareness as a symptom of artistic necessitation, hence conduces to regard. The routine bespeaks habit and lack of concern and impulsion, while the varied bespeaks the aberrational qualities often characteristic of creative process: its unpredictable turns.

The appearance of dominance means that one can feel about the work that "It is in the main or above all such and such (in contrast with being characterless, or nothing in particular)." And the item with a particular thrust or "personality" dominating it is, again, graspable in, and inviting to, attention.

The apparent quality of dominance is also coincident with the potential for looming in awareness with emphatic presence—hereness—which conduces to realization of the object in awareness. By its "taking a firm stand," by its "marked personality" the dominated object tends to intrude upon attention much more than that which seems ephemeral, neither this nor that, and it tends to foster realization of itself by its very appearance, in its having a defined character, in having jelled and not, therefore, appearing as the yet-to-show-up or the indeterminate, to which one cannot as readily attend.

For similar reasons the apparent stability, the balance, of the item increases one's sense of the item's hereness, as the item seems to be "on the current scene," not "becoming" but "arrived," "materialized," here. And so one can go on. If an item shows *continuity* it may be a single

Individual, but without continuity a painting in effect breaks down into several things; figure-and-ground contrasts must be sufficient to yield particularity, but not so great as to divorce figure from ground; i.e., break the continuity, or there will be no *one* figure-and-ground relationship, but rather separate realms, a one-thing here and another back of it, not an integer. For similar reasons, apparent *harmony* of parts is expected.

All of which prompts the assertion that the apparent

design qualities are coincident with and descriptive of those structural characteristics of art objects which usually constitute their especial viability for visual attention.

However, I mentioned in passing that the insistence upon the exhibition of design qualities in art objects, though helpful when read as a symptom of an intuitive grasp of art, is sometimes faulty. Practically, one fault in it is that it often focuses the creator's efforts upon a contriving of structure rather than upon creating the being crying to be born whose structure is indigenous to it. But more important, the insistence upon design qualities as minimal for admissability as art object is theoretically wrong. The potential for gripping and structuring a field of attention must of itself be considered a necessary characteristic of the art object and this potential must not be exclusively identified with those organizational means which *usually* constitute it. If one does make this erroneous identification he becomes confused when works which do not seem to exhibit the design qualities none the less operate as art objects. It should be understood, for example, that works which hold together as a unity only just barely, and hence seem low in design excellence, may be for this reason attention-engaging; they establish a tension between what the viewer is trying to make of the work, i.e., something stable, unified, harmonious, etc., and the provisions available for this making; or they juxtapose structure with haphazardness, and the tension and opposition itself is intriguing, thusly fostering regard status for the object. Also, there are examples of Pop Art where the structure of the work is apparently null and the form itself is changeable (e.g., Claes Oldenberg's *Typewriter*, Plate 10), works in which it is meaningless to speak of "its design." But the very denial of design-as-crystallization, the very emphasis upon softness, amorphousness, can, like

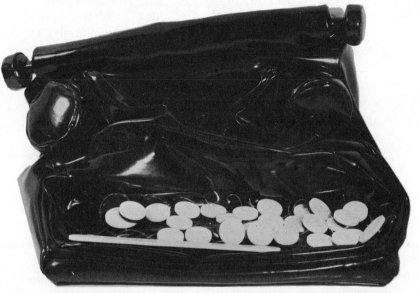

10. Claes Oldenburg, *Soft Typewriter* (1963). Doing the job, binding regard, somehow, is essential—not the design means by which the job is usually done. (Private Collection, Sidney Janis Gallery, New York)

a wrestling match with a greased piglet, by proffering elusiveness be intriguing. Also, when Marcel Duchamp exhibited a metal bottle-drying rack, a snowplow, and a porcelain urinal one saw not only so much shaped metal, and ceramic of known usage but the gesture and posture of the act which proffered these things, and *its* implicit meanings; and the act as well as the sight offered may constitute a potential for fostering regard, without "a design" bearing such meanings at all. And perhaps many a Jackson Pollock canvas seems too much like a slice of a continuum to loom as a bounded, particularized individual; but then these pieces of a continuum foster immersion of the subject within it by gripping means other than the boundedness evident among the usual design qualities. The viability for vision of such works consists, as it were, not so much in their ready visual digestibility as in their potential for stimulating the appetite and making one chew. They exert their hold none the less and so congeal an object–subject conjunction; and, to repeat, the potential for doing this, and not the usual means constituting this potential, is a necessary characteristic of the art object.

In addition to, in structure, being an enticing field for visual attention to live in, a painting tends to conscript regard by presenting something that seems a marvel, whose marvelousness is realizable only while one is seeing the work, and which hence fosters such seeing of it. Namely, it presents a sight which seems in its nature and properties to be one sort of thing while transcending itself to be at the same time quite another sort of thing.

For example, we note that paintings seem to "have a life of their own" while having their dead materiality also in evidence; to say that a great painting is lifeless, though literally true of course, seems false, so conspicuous is the

11. Marcel Duchamp, *Girl with Bedstead* (1916–1917). The given is the thing seen and the gesture of giving "this thing" for regard. Selection, and blurring the modes of give-and-take, as an art act. (Louise and Walter Arensberg collection. Philadelphia Museum of Art)

apparency that while paint is inanimate, it also "comes alive," exhibits vitality.

"Something there is that does not love a wall," begins the famous poem *Mending Wall* by Robert Frost, and therein one is given "wall" that is and remains throughout the poem "stone fence," while at the same time it is and remains throughout the poem "barrier between men" and "residue of outmoded attitudes"; the wall seems to be a plain, material fence and at the same time a lofty symbol while being the concept symbolized; seeming each of these very different things, *evidently,* while remaining the others. And among other things, we find ourselves intrigued by the very manyness of the one-thing Frost gives us; the marvel of something being This *and* That at the same time; its dualism, its living a double (or multiple) life, as it were.

Similarly, one finds of a realistic and insightful portrait of a friend: "This is Joe up there. And I marvel because in a strange way it is reds, greens, browns, whites, paint-stuff, *while* it is still Joe." Indeed, one cannot fully account for the hold a realistic painting exerts upon attention without reference to the marvel of paint being itself and being other also; the marvel of being given that which is still, not given, of seeing a one-thing ("just paint on canvas") which apparently is a two-thing (paint *and* man in one). (See Plate 12.)

And we are intrigued in many abstract works by paint which apparently has a feeling about it or which moves *while* the paint remains stuff which, in fact and evidence, has no feelings in or about it and which remains unmoving. We marvel at a feeling being where it is also not being.

And in "action painting" we marvel at a work seeming spontaneous, natural, while seeming (in its order) some-

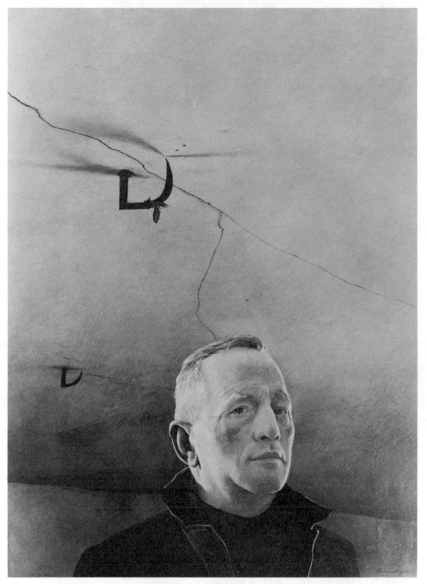

12. Andrew Wyeth, *Karl* (1948). A dualism: "just paint" while "really a man." (Private collection, courtesy M. Knoedler and Co., Inc. Photographed by Brenwasser)

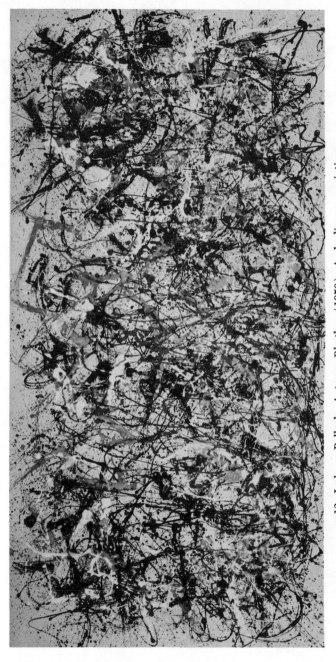

13. Jackson Pollock, *Autumn Rhythm* (1950). A dualism: a painting apparently free, *while* determined. (Metropolitan Museum of Art, George A. Hearn Fund, 1957)

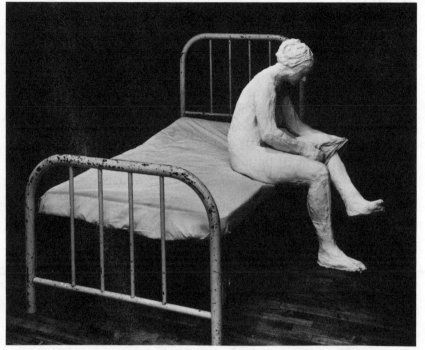

14. George Segal, *Woman on a Bed* (1963). A given which blurs the everyday-perception mode with that of the aesthetic. (Sidney Janis Gallery, New York)

thing that nature's spontaneity and naturalness cannot give; we see a presence that *apparently* is loose and free yet, marvelously, *is* unloose and determined. (See Plates 1, 13.)

Another more recent example: in many works of Pop Art the boundaries between art and everyday life seem blurred, the mode of givenness is unclear, and hence the proper taking posture is uncertain. George Segal places a plaster (art material) nude on a real-life bedstead (Plate 14) and how is one to align oneself toward the construction? As towards a regard-thing? A perception? But intriguing is this very doubleness itself; the work being an art-profference *while* evidently the stuff we run into daily. Our reception attitudes, in being torn between two modes, are hung up; we are in a limbo, or land between accustomed behavioral possibilities. But in so being we are in the art realm; to plant one foot in art and the other elsewhere *for contemplation* of being suspended over a behavioral no-man's-land is an art act, creating another marvel of the art sort. And similarly, beautiful-holy dualisms have long been with us in sacred ikons, as have magic-beautiful ones in totem poles and primitive ritual objects, where "How shall I take it?" questions arise, too, in a manner akin to that just noted.

One must here distinguish between these aesthetic dualisms and illusions, with which they are often erroneously, even if understandably, identified.

What constitutes an illusion? And upon what does the onlooker's sense of marvel depend when confronting an illusion? Consider: the stage illusionist waves a wand and his assistant is floated into the air and we marvel at being given what appears as a single-sided, bare-faced fact—the body is hovering without support and that's that—while this appearance belies what we know must be the case in accordance with necessarily obtaining natural law. We marvel at the adroitness and the convincingness of the lie. And an illusion, to *be* such, must display nothing which would prevent one from taking the presentation as other than what it purports to be on its face. If wires were to be seen supporting the body one would not call what one sees an illusion, because the necessarily obtaining laws in the case would accord with the appearance and hence nothing illusory would be involved.

Now the identification of art with illusion is symptomatic of men's discernment that works of art proffer (at least) two appearances at once, one of which is an impossibility; paint is paint and never has vitality or movement or feeling or personality—though, marvelously, it seems to. But the identification is inaccurate in that the marvelousness of art's dualism lies in the conspicuous *co-incidence and co-appearance*, in art, of the possible with the impossible; in the open declaration of the art object that its (possible) materiality is there to make appear its (impossible) spirituality, whereas the illusion on its face declares falsely that the impossible has occurred and proffers a single lying appearance. In that both stretch beyond simple accordance of raw fact with appearance, aesthetic dualism and illusion (and magic) are alike, but are not identical. (See Plates 13, 15.)

(And, of course, assertions that, say, realistic portraiture [e.g., Plate 12] is more illusionistic than, say, abstract expressionism [Plate 13] are groundless, for both proffer impossibilities coincident with possibilities; flat–deep and dead–alive pairings in the first instance, spontaneous–determined and non-feeling–expressive pairings in the second instance; and on no grounds can one say that one such profference is more illusionistic than the other.)

Incidentally, it is the loss of dualistic regard-conscript-

15. Justin Schorr, *The Audience.* A dualism, when one foot is in reality, and the other in the dream. (Photographed by Walter J. Russell)

ing marvels which accounts for the sometime failure of those works which require elaborate technical means (e.g. electric motors for movement, lights, live actors, theater settings) for their presentation. For the greater the machinery through which aesthetic effects are achieved, the less (literally) marvelous they appear. It seems a wonder when, say, dead paint exhibits qualities of life (movement, feeling, vitality) but, understandably, one is inclined to say "No wonder!" when the massive powers of an elaborate technology produce such effects. When the means are great, "the magic" is gone. The effects achieved in elaborately constructed environments and happenings, e.g. the blurred modes of givenness, the new types of experience proffered, may, as in the Greek festivals or medieval pageants which are the happening's antecedents, justify the sacrifice of the marvelous for their achievement. But this loss may occur without adequate gains of other sorts to compensate for it, and thus one can well understand why some highly sophisticated presentations sometimes fail to bind regard.

Now, such capacities and qualities of art objects as have been rendered do not fully portray their regard-conscripting potentials, for as described an art object might *seem* emptily clever, even inane, whereas *in fact* it is worthy, deserving of attention. From whence might this aspect of merit derive?

On the face of it, the art object seems respectable; even when sportive in manner, gay in tone, light in subject matter and style it is not, apparently, "fooling around." Also, men have sought out and made works of art down through the ages and often at great expense to themselves in time, effort, and neglect of other goods. This apparent respectability and evident value to men leads one to suspect that some substantial and important needs are met by the making and taking of art objects; one would not find something exerting the pull upon and control of lives that art does exert, if all art could afford were trivial pleasure or fun. And because one can, moreover, so readily infer from the appearance of art objects and the characteristics of men how such objects might easily be (serious) need-fulfillers, one is much inclined by the plausibility of the statement to say that they indeed are.

Of what sort of need?

If a painting proffers an image which fulfills in the imagination a repressed wish (e.g., Susanna and the Elders—Plate 16—might satisfy one's voyeuristic wish to spy upon a nude woman) without mitigation by the guilt or consequences entailed in this wish-fulfillment when occurring in everyday life, the object would seem fine, something to be seen. "It feels good and there is nothing bad about it," one might say.[6]

Also, we need not be Platonists to admit that ideals obtain in life, as those forms to which individuals aspire, as projected ultimates of species. And a painting which concretizes such ideals materializes one's otherwise vague and amorphous projections for things-at-their-best, *thereby* seeming good and attention-demanding. (Plate 20.) The good so realized may seem gratuitous rather than food for a hunger one feels, yet reflection reveals that man's appetite for ideality is a persisting one, and that which feeds it would seem good and regard-conscriptive.

Also tending to loom as meritorious would be objects which mean or express something (e.g., a sense of what life feels like) of apparent significance to the viewer. (Plates 7, 17, 19.) Such would seem worthy because identified, typically, with such of our major commitments as concern with the ends, means, and meaning of living.

Also fostering regard for itself by seeming good in

16. Rembrandt, *Susanna and the Elders.* Among other things, a repressed wish vicariously, harmlessly, and hence, innocently fulfilled.
(Marburg-Art Reference Bureau)

17. Meindert Hobbema, *A Woodland Road*. A particular feel of life revealed in the subject and form. (The Metropolitan Museum of Art, Bequest of Mary Stillman Harkness, 1950)

18. Mark Rothko, *No. 10* (1950). Not the import it carries, but rather the desirable event it enables. (The Museum of Modern Art, New York. Gift of Philip C. Johnson. Photographed by Geoffrey Clements)

19. Picasso, *Night Fishing at Antibes* (1939). Art as stepping stone to new awareness, a means of transcendence. (Collection, The Museum of Modern Art, New York. Mrs. Simon Guggenheim Fund. Photographed for the Museum by Soichi Sunami)

vision would be the item which tends to foster *behavior* of a sort itself profoundly gratifying even if the object, but for this behavior-prompting capacity, seems unexceptional. A country road by moonlight may not seem, intrinsically, especially good, but when one finds that experience of such puts him in a gratifying frame of mind one may find the good inherent in the object inseparable in experience from its intrinsic merits. It is understandable, then, why one finds meritorious paintings which seem largely atmospheric in effect, e.g., a misty Chinese landscape, good as a catalyst of the good event, not for what they contain but for what they precipitate. (See Plate 18.)

And looming as extraordinarily good would be the object which catalyzes not just any good frame of mind but a condition in which an instance of psychic growth occurs, one which offers a stepping-stone to an expanded consciousness.[7] The "real eye-opener," the object "alive with meaning" in so being seems good, much as a light to a searcher or a hand-up to a climber does. (Plate 19.)

Now, these several functions (and others one might cite) image-proffering objects could fulfill in the life of mentality, and through such fulfillment and gratification could seem so good in and for regard, when presented in a visually viable and marvelous structure, as to make this reception for it seem obligatory. Indeed, each of the cited functions has been put forth by a great philosopher, and with much supporting evidence, as being of paramount importance in art. And this evidence cannot be dismissed, for if it is insufficient to demonstrate that a particular function is as important as its exponent believes, it is evidence which none the less points to the sometime, somehow presence of this function in the realm of art. And though one does not want to be overly open in his welcome to differing beliefs, one feels inclined by the weight of these several philosopher's cases to find variety characterizing art's functions.

And this view is also urged by the variety among extant art objects; one wishes a pluralistic cumulative outlook to afford one relief from the task of considering a Van Gogh, a Raphael Madonna, a pre-historic cave-drawing, and a Japanese calligraphic drawing to be "essentially alike in function," a task any single-function theory urges.

Furthermore, with appreciative phenomena defined, such functional pluralism does not become precluded as non-definitive, unstructured, meaningless eclecticism. That which makes an object an instance of the art sort of thing is definable as its especial potential, which is held in common with other items of its sort, for prompting a particular defined sort of goings-on—the aesthetic sort. And this allows one to say that this potential may be variously comprised; so saying does not make the art object anything-at-all. Nor is the assertion non-exclusive; the sort of functions art serves are not any, and every, one. For example, we do not want tools or truths or divine revelations to just be with in regard, nor is every human need served by the holding up for contemplation of some regardable.

But now, in theory what *amounts* of the cited types of regard-conscripting factors would constitute a sufficiency for mustering visual attention?

Everyone lives in an economy of time and value and knows his own finitude; and to be looking at painting A is not to be looking at painting B or eating a gratifying meal or helping a neighbor or doing any other good thing, and this is obvious to men. Hence, for painting A to have the potential for being conscriptive of awareness it must seem not merely somewhat gratifying, viable, and dualistic, but so very much so, that, given one's current needs and what experience has taught him he may expect of his days, the painting will win out in the competition of worthy demands upon his attention. To claim, then, that any amount of the regard-conscripting factors cited is sufficient to constitute an attention-mustering potential would be wrong. And in fact, who finds binding, say, a *somewhat expressive* painting?

Is this potential in each case made large enough, then, by being a multifold aggregate of functional capacities and visual marvels? Many works of art afford a dense amalgam of many need-fulfilling capacities, all of which together probably account for much of the items' claim upon attention. When, for example, one appreciates a Michelangelo fresco (Plate 20) he is of course aware of a unitary ineffable feeling rather than a batch of function-fulfillments, but evident in the work and in one's experience of it is support for the belief that a wish-fulfillment *and* an idealization of a sort *and* a keen sense of life's struggles well-expressed all fostered one's response to it. Moreover, in addition to the massing of powers such an amalgam provides, the item which serves many functions thereby leaves no one functional capacity conspicuous as the item's reason-for-being. The object, then, in seeming good apparently exists to some avail, but one not namable. And this apparent purposelessness, which all the while seems to be of service, tends to be most intriguing. And this situation is apprehendable and appreciable only *in* regard. Here, a multiple need-fulfilling capacity, even if not great in its several parts or in simple sum, would in its very multiplicity tend to constitute sufficiency for fostering regard.

However, one or two aesthetic powers may alone also be factors adequate in amount for constituting a regard-conscriptive potential. The ideality of a Goya (Plate 21)

20. Michelangelo, *The Creation of Man.* Wish-fulfillment, *or* idealization, *or* expression? Or rather, the dense fulfiller of many functions? (Alinari-Art Reference Bureau)

21. Goya, *A City on a Rock.* Its expressiveness would alone suffice to conscript our regard. (The Metropolitan Museum of Art. Bequest of Mrs. H. O. Havemeyer, 1929. The H. O. Havemeyer Collection)

is difficult to trace, while the expressiveness is evident; and this expressiveness is probably the functional capacity which counts most in, and suffices for, mustering contemplation. It is not true that inevitably the more good qualities the painting has, the better it will bind attention. Sometimes to add, say, ideal-realizing loveliness to expressive brute-power may vitiate the latter, sacrificing thusly the binding effect of the extreme standpoint and in all losing more than is gained. In sum, then, I am saying that an object-subject wedding occurs when, in type and amount, the object brings to the subject enough that is intriguing and worthwhile to make engagement seem obligatory. "Enough" is here contingent upon the man, his days, his needs, his time and place in history, and the extent to which the object meshes with these. Sufficiency is not *theoretically* determinable (though its constituents are discussable).

But one may object that this leaves the regard-conscripting potential as wholly conditional and occasional. And I would now amplify and argue this point further, by citing a common occurrence.

Jones and Smith are looking at the same painting. They both believe that a work of art is an object which has the potential for making aesthetic value realizable in experience, and their apprehensions of what constitutes such value and the degree of it necessary for aesthetic adequacy are identical. But to Jones the painting looms as a work of art and to Smith it looms only as a mere painting, respectable perhaps, but no more. At first only two possible explanations of the Jones–Smith predicament occur to us: (1) Smith is not realizing aesthetic value in his experience of the work because little or none is there to be realized. Jones is only concocting or projecting value into his experience with a little assistance from a work itself lacking art quality. (2) Jones is realizing the value the painting in fact proffers for realization. Smith is failing to realize any aesthetic potential but that does not prove the object lacks it; after all, it may not be realized because of Smith's insensitivity or a blinding prejudice, and may still inhere in the object. Were Smith and Jones to debate the virtues of the painting they would argue over what both construed to be a matter of unconditional fact, namely, over whether the painting does or does not make art value realizable in experience, to whatever extent both deem sufficient for laudability as art.

But a third possibility arises if we note that while the potential discussed is a special capacity to do certain things in and for awareness, each man's awareness differs from that of other men even when the extent and quality of their experience, sensitivity, intellect, and openness is equal among them, for their equalness is not their sameness. The possibility is that the painting *has* the potential for conscripting Jones' attention and not that of his equal, Smith; and the painting *is* a work of art because being so entails having the potential for conscripting *some* men's regard at some times (whether or not these men in fact realize this value made available to them), and does not entail having this potential for a *universal* man. And this would be to say that the potential for conscripting regard is constituted of qualities and capacities still more varied than heretofore described herein, in its consisting in each instance of the potential for conscripting some of a highly varied lot of consciousnesses. Each work of art needs to have the exact qualifications for doing a particular sort of job (fostering appreciative situations), but upon different sort of subjects at different times and each may hence differ greatly from others engaged in the same task.

Several considerations beg us to admit this view. For

one thing, it does often appear that men of *equivalent* (though different) sensitivities, freedom from prejudice, liberality, experience, and education are repeatedly in the Smith–Jones predicament, even with renowned, time-honored paintings, and one wonders why the Smiths cannot, despite all effort, realize the work's value if art value is indeed something universally realizable to all men of great aesthetic sensitivity and openness. Usually we see as one of *Smith's* limitations an apparent absence of the apparatus for realizing the painting's potential, since the latter is presumed to be universally available. But it seems equally sensible to say, "This painting is equipped to structure, conscript, and reward Jones' awareness, but, though great in art quality, it lacks the equipment to do this job on Smith, superlative appreciator though he is. Yet this limitation of the painting does not disqualify it as an art object, for sufficiency as art does not entail sufficiency to operate as art for all art-appreciative men." One is, I am saying, urged to hold this view for its accordance with the occurrent differences of response among such men to a work of art, in that it does not make one choose between labeling either the painting or the man as adequate, when both seem to be.

And this contingency-view seems supported by theory. If men are indeed engaged by an object and find it valuable partly because it has the capacity to fulfill their wishes, concretize their ideals, organize their chaotic experiences, provide steppingstones to an expanded consciousness, etc., then theoretically it must require different sorts of objects to engage different men. For each man's particular wishes, ideals, direction of transcendence, etc. are not consistent with those of other men. The bucolic scene that is enticing because restful and familiar to one tired farmer is necessarily repulsive because restful and familiar to his excitement-seeking neighbor; Ruben's type of woman makes ideal-concretization realizable in the experience of some men, but not necessarily for Cranach (and men of his constitution) for whom it cannot even have a potential value. And the painting which offers Jones value by affording him a steppingstone cannot make this value even findable by Smith if he is travelling in another direction. Indeed that steppingstone has no potential even for Jones once he has crossed this stream, never to return. (And have we not all outgrown paintings once held dear?) It would seem, then, that a sufficient potential for fostering art-appreciative situations would be comprised, in theory as in practice, of various and diverse constituents; a potential real and of a particular sort, but occasional in being contingent upon the man and circumstances in the aesthetic confrontation.

Is there no aesthetic virtue, then, that a work of art makes discernable by all keen men?

It would be possible for a person confronting a painting which did not have the potential for acting in his awareness as an art object, to recognize that aspect of it to which one may point with the terms "validity" and "logical integrity." One may see evidence of certain givens or "premises" in the painting; e.g., rhythms or motifs strongly stated, which were apparently made to co-operate with other very different givens, to yield a whole, comprised of the varied factors, which embraces, and is constituted of, them all. The working out of the thrusts (literally and figuratively) of the givens in an orderly way may be appreciable by all keen observers, much as all may appreciate the interplay of teams, goals, and rules in a football game, which form a field structured for attention over time and space, though one may not be entranced by this particular game or its participants. Such appreciation of

"validity" is usually part of an aesthetic experience
(though not a distinguishing part—it is more prominent
in theory-appreciation), but it is also less than such an
experience, though more widely available to the viewers
of a particular painting.

In effect, then, I have said that the statement, "This is a
work of art" can be made about Painting A objectively—
i.e., in the sense of reflecting what is indeed the case—
only if one is therewith classifying the painting as, say, an
art-work rather than a tool-work; or, if one is therewith
citing a record of instances in which aesthetic value was
realized from it, stating in effect a statistic reflective of its
past behavior and its merits to the extent that they are
inferable from that behavior. This does not depict the
virtues of art objects as qualities foisted on things by
whimsical subjects; again, the potentials for fostering aesthetic goings-on are several and are variously comprised
but are none the less definable job-doing capacities, which
inhere in objects. An art potential is really existant and
not just subjectively fancied as real, though obtaining
only in situations where its strengths can indeed be capa-
cious.

Now earlier I suggested that not only do aesthetic
goings-on occur as described but that they are, in experience as well as in theory, distinctive: not identifiable or
identified with any other sort of phenomenon. Let me
briefly argue this view, an argument which is necessary if
my description is to be definative. I will argue that not
only is the art object definable as that which has an especial potential for inciting the aesthetic sort of goings-on
(now defined) but that in daily experience objects indeed
receive the laudatory label "work of art" when, and because, this potential is realized in a situation identified as
aesthetic in nature; that the item is taken to be an art

object not through cognition or apprehension of a function or property common to art objects and hence denominative of them, nor through the workings of such unbe-
knownst to the viewer, but through the item being object
of an experience whose characteristics mark it as of the
aesthetic sort.

I have already indicated the factors which, in experience and theory, differentiate art from such givens as
illusions, "mere paintings," suppositions, and routine perceptions; other modes need not detain us since they are
not confused and confusable with the aesthetic. However,
religious objects loom as "to be attended to," and one's
attention is gripped when participating in a game. What
in theory (then in experience) differentiates aesthetic,
religious, and game situations?

The differentiating factors are not those of property
differences among objects involved in the respective
realms. So Wittgenstein argued, stating that there is no
property that is a common denominator of games; Morris
Weitz then convincingly extended the argument to say
the equivalent thing about art objects.[8] Indeed, no one has
managed to state such denominators.[9] However, it is the
different conditions obtaining in situations in these realms
that differentiates each from the others—the modes of
give-and-take, the nature of the situations involved—
which are discernable not only upon reflection but also in
daily life.

For example, a *game* is, for one thing, a situation which
evidently stems from positing. One posits that certain
goals really are one's objectives and that certain rules
govern as by right and necessity, and one takes up a
posit-ion, of mind as well as body, doing so in a way
conspicuous to him. And that which is posited on the face
of it seems, unlike some other posited structures, not good

as a possibly true picture of one's actual fate or as a wish-fulfillment. Rather, the game's rules, procedures, and goals loom as lacking in any intrinsic goodness, and the system posited, while ordered and self-perpetuating, seems clearly pointless, to no avail. But its value appears as anticipatable, that is, realizable after the game is made to exist experientially. That is why one justifies making and taking the givens of a game not by pointing to the justice of its laws or the value of realizing its goals as such, but by pointing to the *yield* of living in the game field. "Take part," one says, "it will be fun, it will do you good."

The *religious* given, however, looms on the face of it as a commanding Power, as directed to and binding upon one's actual destiny and conduct, and it is taken in a stance of deep concern and awe. And this sort of taking seems "only realistic." The necessity of having our thinking accord with reality prompts our reception attitude rather than a hope of future good to be realized; and no positing is involved. Nor may one ignore the given; its numina, for whatever causes or reasons, seems a present reality and evidently should be cognized as such.

One can then see a few ways in which in theory, art, game, and religious phenomena differ (and can see that because the differences are simple and directly intuitable, they may be in experience differentiated). The art viewer, unlike the game participant, posits nothing. And he knows this directly; he just lets be the image given him, evidently without taking up a position. Also, goodness seems to reside in the art object when appreciated, while the goodness of the game looms as anticipatable or as remembered from past experience. But although in this appearance of intrinsic goodness the art object is like the religious object, they are unlike in that the art object is evidently binding only upon regard, a thing to be just seen, but not as the religious object binding upon conduct or one's decision for one's self. And, in art a charming fantasy may act in awareness to make one say, "I ought to stay in this fine world (of the canvas)"; but it does not say, "This *is* the world," as a religious item may. An art object may change men's lives but it does not seem *made* to do so; not given as something to be considered as a changer, as is a religious object. Nor is it so taken. And the art object seems marvelous and impressive but its marvelousness looms as the outcome of an amazing feat (we admire the man who can work such marvels), not as identical with the seat of miracles, holy as the religious object seems.

And perhaps differentiation in actual experience is most conspicuous in those instances when art, games, and religion are apparently distorted one into another; for by our conspicuous awareness that a distortion has indeed occurred we point to the fact that we have a conception, disturbed by the distortion, of what such situations normally and properly involve. And we point with our disturbance to the content of our conception of such situations. For example, one sometimes says of a professional baseball player, "He makes of baseball a business," indicating that, though the profit motive often *accrues* to games, the yearning for profit is not characteristic of the game stance. And one sometimes says of the dilettante painter that he makes a game of art, indicating that, although a pleasure-motive may accompany art, it is not part of the art-posture (of making what seems called for, necessary). And one is disturbed when what appears to one as Holy Writ is taken only as poetry, i.e. art, for although aesthetic values often accompany religious items, to take a sacred thing only for these values and not as life-controlling and soul-conscripting is to assume the wrong reception stance. In each instance to be disturbed at a *wrong* stance or

other wrong conditions in a situation is to indicate our
experiential awareness of the right, the norm, of situations
in these realms. All of which supports the assertion that
art appreciative situations are theoretically identifiable as
such, and are differentiable in daily life from other sorts of
goings-on, and that the object in such experience, however various such objects are, are rightly identifiable as objects of art.

Now, the case for the view that art objects are indeed
identified as such when, and because, they are objects of
situations known by the involved subjects to be aesthetic
situations may be challenged. Yet this is the view I would
hold to more strenuously than any other stated heretofore.
That is, I readily accept that one's discernment of the
phenomenology of appreciative experience may well
differ from that stated above, and one's beliefs as to what
constitutes the art object's potential for looming as it does
may well contradict mine, but I would insist that the art
object is identified as such in experience by men's awareness of the distinctive phenomenology of aesthetic experience (however this is best described) and the reflection
of this awareness upon the object. But the case for this
view depends upon choosing the best among alternative
views, none of which is completetly destructible. I state,
then, only that no one has cited an art-denominative property or function or cohesive group of properties that
could mark an object, by appearance or effect, as an art
object—none which would be convincing to the community of men who reflect on this matter. Nor can the fact of
life be denied that objects do achieve the honorific label
"work of art" under circumstances which make it difficult
to view the labelling act as "purely subjective"; some sort
of cognition of a reality seems involved. If these two views
of how art objects become called such are rejected (this

rejection is suggested but is not inescapable) the one I submit seems the only entertainable one remaining. And it is a plausible one; for I have shown that art appreciative experience is discernable as such in awareness, and that men's behavior indicates that this discernment is made. And I have indicated how objects with properties and functions oft noted as characteristic of things long taken to be art objects (though not denominative of them) could incite the phenomena described. The model presents a system that could work and could be now working.

Also, as stated earlier, this view is open for continued changes in our conception of an art object's properties, in that it defines the sort of occurrences in art but does not limit the means by which these occurrences may be fostered; and obviously changes in these means occur often. The pattern of accommodation of this model to changes in artistic practices follows the facts of aesthetic life, and this congruence of theoretic with practical change supports the model. That is, expression theory is shaken by paintings which do not so much *mean* (anything) but *act* (as say, sunlight on flesh acts but does not mean). But, as noted before, in art experience men confront objects and if their experience seems to them of the art sort, they say, "Though the object's properties are unlike those of other art objects, it must be art; I'll change my conception of such properties because I'm unable to deny the fact of my experience." And this is the pattern of growth of my model; to identify the aesthetic experience and inquire into its possible incitors, allowing, even assuming, change among these.

In all, these considerations support, even if they cannot prove, my case for identification of the art object through phenomenological researches and inferences from the findings; and they are checked by studies of the objects

labelled as art, the process exemplified above, whether the
process is well-used here or not.

And now let us ask a few questions about how and why
such objects come into the world, thus considering the
artist at work and the object worked on from another
standpoint: that of its maker.

2

On the Artist at Work

THE FEW PAGES OF THIS CHAPTER ARE OF COURSE NOT PUR-
ported to be an extensive or otherwise ambitious discussion
of how and why artists work. The essays only undertake a
few small tasks in this area.

First among these is a plea for a particular frame of
mind in which to receive substantive claims about the
artist's behavior.

THE PAINTER'S CONDUCT AS SYSTEM OF FORCES

Ask a literate and reflective artist why he paints as he
does and his answer will probably be a long string of
phrases marked by the words "Because—and because—
and because." That is, he will display the cognition that
the causes of, and reasons for, his painting conduct are
numerous and complex. And he would admit, furthermore, that though he names many forces in citing those he
knows of, there are probably still others he cannot name.

Thusly, he admits to the even greater complexity of the factors shaping his acts.

Yet, to the task of explaining the artist's conduct, most men—artists among them—bring a simplistic mode of thought. One hears, "He did this because of that." Depth psychology has not much changed this pattern. It only says that the causes of his doing "this" may not be overt, reasonable, or knowable; but they are still of a particular type, e.g., sexual; or of a particular order, e.g., causes emergent from (all) aspects of one's history or personality. Such thinking does not accord with artists' experience. As an alternative I suggest we consider the creative act as the resultant of a dynamic, changing, complex system of forces, with numerous sub and sub-sub systems within it; some personal and some not. And this (creative) system, must itself be seen as a sub-system within a larger whole: that of the human being, among others, in an existential situation. Also, the entirety must be considered theoretically (though not practically) comprehendible *as,* and only as, *system* (and investigatable by researchers only through systems analysis), and that it must be held in thought *as system.* Let me further display this suggestion first through metaphorical means.

At any moment the life process of a tree may be thought of as a system with numerous sub-systems within it. Within these sub-systems numerous forces with direction (i.e., vectors,) interact, thus yielding resultants which then act as vectors in the total system. The shape and "behavior" of the tree at any moment, then, is the resultant of vectors from these sub-systems as they reinforce, counter, deflect, re-form, cancel each other, within each sub-system, and as they reach out to others within the total. For example: there is for each tree, a light system, a soil (nutrient, rooting) system, a climatic system, etc. Some several forces within, say, the climatic system, may buttress each other, each making for growth (e.g., much sunlight and much rainfall). Some several may have countered each other, and forces within other sub-systems; (e.g., the soil-nutrient one) may not only have yielded a soil which is, in result, a growth vector, but is especially reinforcing of one or several vectors within the climatic system (e.g., a soil that *with* much rainfall is especially conducive to growth). The resultant, the tree, is not the effect of a single cause, and it is not a mirror of the seething systems of forces at work. It is their outcome, a yield which does not necessarily reveal all its determinants. And because the sub-systems are manifold and themselves have sub-sub-systems within them (e.g. insect systems within soil) and because, most importantly, in time each changes—perhaps evenly, perhaps in spurts —the outcome is apparently beyond calculation and human prediction. Yet there is a law in this process, not a simple cause–effect linear law, but rather the law of organic determination. And while apparently one cannot, practically, do a systems analysis of a tree, it is at least possible to think of a tree as system (as men are doing of cities), and to analyze that portion of its life which interests one while maintaining a sense of the whole life and the place of the portion within it.

The artist creating in his particular circumstances, I suggest, can likewise be considered as a system of forces, within which are sub-systems. Some examples: the persistent psychological needs of the artist as a man (with its own numerous sub-sub-systems), needs for the object and for what the act of making it does for him, the "thrusts" of art materials, the many criss-crossing currents of the creator's previous artistic experience, recent art history with its emphases and lessons pushing this way and that, belief and feeling systems relative to his world, and so on. The act and the appearance of the finished work is the resultant of such forces, *all* of which, by pushing and not pushing, forming and deforming, *caused* this resultant, which is not their mirror but their outcome.

In addition: to emphasize some forces in order to provide a convenient conceptual handle for creative acts, or because they seem essential or central, and to ignore others because they seem marginal, is to ignore the fact that centrality varies from case to case. More importantly, this is to adopt a mode of evaluation certain to obscure the process by which art acts and objects are yielded, a process of determination wherein every force counts. It is to say that, as it were, the heart matters, when in fact art grows from the whole body, and to dispense with any part of it in theory is to lie about what actually determined the growth.

And if, on its face, this seems a strange view, let us rush to observe that the multiplicity of art's determinants and the seething, multitudinous force–counterforce effect is everywhere evident in art. Jackson Pollock's well-known spontaneous and intuitive approach wherein personal unpremeditated urges, (themselves likely the resultant of a complex psychic sub-system) seem foremost, at the heart of the process, still contained within it, as he said, a general idea of the sort of thing he was about to make; i.e., a degree of intention (the resultant of a belief or cognitive sub-system). Academic artists—who approached their canvasses only after each inch of the painting-to-be had been studied, plotted, and composed in drawings—still, in these drawings, arranged, accepted, and edited, on grounds which were, despite their theories, as ultimately mysterious or irrational as those of their Romantic opponents who advocated irrationality. No simple cause–effect relationship or simple Gestalt determined their works. Even such insistent painter-theorists as Josef Albers (Plate 22) and Mondrian (Plate 23), whose series of rectilinear works declare a control solely by intention, still have their work influenced by the qualities of and their skill with paint, and by whatever are the forces within the art scene and themselves, which in result prompt their very intentions. Delacroix believed in Romanticism, Courbet in Realism; but, beliefs notwithstanding, Delacroix is in some respects (pre-planning) academic and Courbet is (in his self-glorification) Romantic. Why? Such deviations from singularity are not due to a compromised will, or frustration, or seduction of virtue by evil; rather, I am suggesting, in the simplest creative situation, many systems of forces are at work, and so the art act and object is an outcome of not a single thrust and hence single-faced but of the interaction of many vectors.

Also, this suggestion that creation includes a variety of forces operating in the manner described accords well with, and is buttressed by, those occurrences of dualisms in the appearances of art objects that we noted before. The lure and, indeed, the necessity of exploiting the physical characteristics of paint *while* intending to portray Mr. Brown yields the paint-while-man dualism of the realistic portrait; any spot on the canvas is the result of at least these two determinants, and exhibits this duality. The slash of the abstract expressionist's brush is impelled by the desire for apparent spontaneity *and* the need to make the paint go in precisely the right place (while appearing "natural") and to make it hold together with the rest of the canvas, and thusly is yielded the free-while-determined double-life effect; and so on.

And the suggestion accords well with the peculiar appearance (oft noted and soon to be described) of creative

22. Josef Albers, *Homage to the Square: "Ascending."* Even programmatic works are the result of many vectors. (Whitney Museum of American Art, New York. Photographed by Oliver Baker Associates, Inc.)

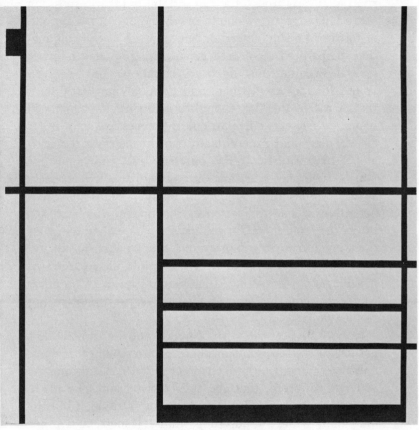

23. Mondrian, *Composition in White, Black, and Red* (1936). An icon of order. The wonder of the man on the tightrope who need go nowhere and carry nothing, but need only stay aloft to amaze us. (Collection, The Museum of Modern Art, New York. Gift of the Advisory Committee. Photographed for the Museum by Soichi Sunami)

directives in conduct. Their "glow," their apparent necessitation and rightness, their unsuitability for transposition
into a language, urges one to see them not as a response to
or mirror of a single need or question but as the conjunction of many. To point to my meaning: if one is given
several simultaneous algebraic equations and is given
values for factors in them, and then solving for X finds
that $X = 3.5$, this 3.5, though not intrinsically fine, will
seem rather special, particularly necessary—no other
answer fits—and exceptionally worthy because it and it
alone, marvelously, is the outcome and climax of this
(one's) complex situation. A creative directive appears
as it does because, given the many systems of forces
operative in one's experience, the image which constitutes the fulfillment, crossroads, and embodiment of
their concurring resultants must seem necessitated and
remarkably worthy, and, with such multiplicity, untrans-
posable into a single-faced language. I know of no other
way to explain this appearance that seems as convincing
as this view.

Now to suggest this turn of mind contributes little that
is substantive to discussions on creative conduct. It does,
however, admonish that artistic experience be recognized
and not distorted, that the substantive claims be made
modestly and seen as fragmentary. For example, it bids us
note that, while Freud, Jung, Rank, Jaspers, and other
great students of human behavior have each made cases
for a motive force in creative conduct, the evidence each
presents does not dispel that of the others and, as one
looks about him, the motives they cite each seem important and actually operative. Moreover, knowing artists
makes one believe that the importance of one sort of
motive vis-à-vis another is a shifting idiosyncratic thing;
therefore assigning priority seems impossible. Each claim

presents a fragment of the truth, and each is awry only
when it claims to be all of the truth, because there is no
evidence that there is only one art root in the psyche and
its dynamics, and much evidence to indicate that there
are many.

I have been saying that if one cares to hold creative
conduct as being explicable, this may be done only by
granting in mind each force constituting it—each within
and each without the personality—its due weight and
thrust; although in practice one cannot tell the whole
truth about a creative act, so complex and unfathomable
is it, one can recognize that nothing less than this whole
really explains the causality of the shape of the act.

The suggestion that creative conduct be held in mind as
a system may be so general and metaphoric as to be
useless to researchers. To artists, perhaps, it will foster—
justifiably, I think—the feeling that this conduct is, to the
extent and in the manner of organismic life, lawful. And
this sense that law obtains, however covertly and uncita-
bly, may be very useful.

ON THE SURFACE OF CREATIVE CONDUCT

Next I try not to display fully the surface of creative
conduct—it is too varied for such to be possible—but
rather to find, within and despite the variety, a pattern
which coheres and makes a kind of sense; that is, further
grounds for a sense that law obtains in artistic life. The
display also tends to recommend further the frame of
thought suggested above, and helps us move on to specific
issues of interest to artists.

To begin with the obvious, at some time during creative
behavior—not always at its outset—the creator experiences the desire to make something loom as a "thing."

He is not content to maintain phantasms, urges, notions, feelings as such; these seem unsatisfyingly inchoate and uncrystallized, without coherent identity, insubstantial. He wants to make something which exhibits not necessarily materiality but cohesiveness, individuality, presence. (In this sense a theory is a Thing, while the theorist's musings prior to crystallization in the theory are not.) This desire to make a "thing" seems inextricable from our very conception of creating; to create, in the honorific and marveling sense in which we use the word in the arts, means to make a being be, to make a "this thing" existant where heretofore this individual was not. We intuitively cognize that to make newly existant "mere stuff" out of old stuff is not what we mean by creating (nor, of course, does creating entail making something out of literally nothing). Creating entails the establishment of a present, cohesive, identity, an individual which in the plastic arts shows up as an object. It may begin with an urge for, not an object, but action of a particular sort. However, at *some* time, what the creator experiences is not merely the urge to do this or to "make something" but to make some being be.

Moreover, the item which the creator feels he wants to make existant as an object seems to him that which *ought* to be made to so loom; one feels it is incumbent upon him, it is his obligation, to create it. His urge seems not mere willfulness but something which exercises rightful sovereignty over him. To this Nietzsche and Jung testified, and Ghiselin also so concludes from the many creative-persons' comments he gathered in his fine compendium.

More often it (the creative beginning) defines itself as no more than a sense of self-surrender to an inward necessity inherent in something larger than the ego and taking precedence over the established order.[1]

Also testifying to the apparently rightful sovereignty of the creative intimation is the war sometimes waged in artists' minds between that which appears as two sovereign goods; e.g., between the urge to create and the obligation to do a family duty. Such a war exists *as* it does, that is, as *between goods* and not between *good* and *evil* because the impulsion to create is not felt as a mere appetite or a highly desirable pleasure or an uncontrollable aspiration (except by those who romanticize it), or as a "mad compulsion," an evil; rather it is felt as an urgent call from that which *deserves* to be heeded, a call seeming deserving even when appearing as less deserving than some other demand.

Though often lacking exactness, a creative urge appears as a somewhat coherent directive, a fairly particularized intimation of a direction to search in, of a movement to make, or of the sort of thing one is to make exist. Perhaps Jarrett goes too far when he writes:

When a creator needs to express himself, this is not just a need in general, a kind of abstract hunger; no, he needs to express *this*, this very special something.[2]

But the excitation of mind and spirit the artist undergoes does at least appear to have a "core" within its (sometime) vagueness, to be "at heart" or "essentially" a directive to do thus-and-so. A painter may begin with the desire to "dance" with paint on canvas, or to assault a surface, or to "fool around with colors"; he only *ends* if somewhere during his dancing or whatever he finds a particularized direction in which to move; finds, often with a tinge of excitement, the sort of thing his act and object is to become, and the act and its object relate to each other to an end increasingly clear.

The artist, I say, has the right-feeling desire to (literally and figuratively) "materialize" something intimated, but materialize this—*as what?* As, say, a tool he needs? No, something good is crying to be made (just) holdable in regard; and eventually the artist works on the item as a man impelled and guided by what sight-fabrication and his need for engaging in the sight-fabricating act entails. To point by contrast, he does not feel the need to make something one can find believable or contestable or supposable; or something one can "have around," as a rug, or wallpaper, is "around." He tests the image's possibilities only as a regardable, a sight, for *as* such does it call for realization.

Also, in creating there is personal excitement, awe, trepidation, involvement with the vision presented and the situation one is in, and yet, as oft noted, there is dispassionate aloofness. This apparent contradiction again points to art's peculiar mode of experience; even these affective conditions seem proffered to be savored, tasted, regarded, rather than managed, judged, acted upon, as one does with perception-provoked feelings. They, as the image, are in art's neutral mode. The artist as he works accepts dispassionately, while others strenuously cope with, the givenness of his givens, be they sights, violent feelings, paints, or whatever. He "lets be" the fact of the appearance of what is at hand, and its operations and qualities; turmoil or calm, aloofness or closeness may show up in his situation. Its showing up is not rejected or welcomed, but taken as given.

And this stance is artistically effective because it allows one to be especially responsive to one's urges, to follow their lead, and to make especially good contact with visual material *as sights*. Because of his non-analytical neutrality, the artist, as does the Zen adept, experiences objects in their "suchness." For example, the drawing student is implored to learn to see and draw, not "a leg" (not a concept, or one's conception of a limb) but "that flesh and bone over there," "this thing as it is experienced." The artist deals not with "red," "yellow," "blue," the idea of a color or a category of color, but "this pigment" as it "feels" in the awareness. And his (often notorious) willingness to move along with his feelings—accepting them as givens when other men reject, magnify, ignore, or analyze them—enables him to concretize that which is right *for* feelings. He undergoes the movements and rhythms of his painting, feels its unity or lack of it, and, being fully responsive, much as is a boxer on the balls of his feet, he is ready to move and is best able to realize what needs realization. Indeed, much of what is called "artistic maturation" is the achievement of this stage of development wherein one's wisdom, knowledge, skills, feelings, intentions, ideas, are all integral in the person at the time of creating, and one performs, not necessarily "spontaneously," but with a nature-like inevitability and directness.

Also, one may readily understand why experiencing the artist's posture is in and for itself desired. It seems very fine indeed to be swept up by aims and urges which seem to seek one out, which inflame one's enthusiasms, and which seem so worthy as to be obligatory; and it seems fine to follow such impetuses by means which not only realize one's goals but which in the act of doing the realizing nourish and accelerate and reward one's efforts. One's subjectivity seems merged with one's overt behavior and the object one is constructing, integrated in a give-and-take with it. Struggle is often involved but one is "in tune" with a world, and this seems a good way to be.

The actual work of creation proceeds in different cases not in any one manner, but in each case, I would submit, with the internal logic of operational systems of forces searching, as it were, for their final resultant. The artist as he progresses in a work is typically locked in an ever more restrictive deterministic situation, wherein the emerging thing calling for realization rules out numerous otherwise admissible possibilities and intimates what is required if "this thing" is to be nurtured into being. The blank canvas tells one not at all what to do, but then one's idea or vision intimates the identity of the thing to be realized or the approach which of itself seems right and good and promises such intimation. And, then, early or late, as the skeleton or keynote of this identity appears on canvas, it sets requirements. Any specific stroke or area of paint usually must fulfill numerous functions and is determined by the variegated need; it must, say, define a place in space, help shape a depicted object, be right as part of a color organization, continue a movement, all to make of the whole the thing desired. And as these requirements become increasingly crystallized they more and more direct conduct, until the last stroke, it appears (whether in fact so or not), need be thus-and-so; just this and nothing else will do. One feels one cannot do other if one is to fulfill the specific determinants operating in this situation, this locus in time and space. Happily, working in the peculiar stance of the artist, one does not "decide" what to do next but rather the painting, and himself as felt, are operative in awareness, the forces *thrust* and yield directives as to what to do, flowing together in a way which seems natural and inevitable (whether in fact so or not).

As might be gathered from my earlier suggestions, the pluralism of this view does not imply that creating entails or even usually involves the equal representation of all the forces that obtain in a creative situation, that no one or group of them are dominant. If an artist is the epitome of the emotional Romantic it is usually "interior" forces

which are the major determinants of his painting. If he is
a classicist following the lure and the discipline of a vision
of beauty or an ideal of formal excellence in the "out
there" then it is demands exerted apparently from without which act as the major force in the creative situation,
determining his yield to a much larger measure than that
of the Romantic. For some men the productive act as such
is so rewarding that the object developing seems subordi-
nate to the feel of the process. But even the Classicist may
be seen as fitting in this organismic model of creative
behavior when the demands of the ideal and the artist's
self-effacing discipline are seen still as only forces, albeit
large ones, in a multiforce situation.

INTENTIONS

Implicit in this discussion is the question of the role and
effect of intentions, stated wants, aesthetic beliefs, and
resolutions in creative conduct and its yield. This role
seems to vary greatly in different cases, is often subtle,
and is subject to much misapprehension. For example,
many of our contemporaries stand so openly before their
work that it is loose talk to say that their finished paintings (in fact or apparently) are or are not what they
"wanted," because it is part of their outlook not to try to
fulfill a pre-conceived want, not to intend but to discover
their want through action and appraisal of action's results.
But certainly other men intend very strongly and make
paintings which consistently exemplify a program, and it
seems foolish to assert that, because one believes that
many forces interact to determine creative conduct, these
artists could not, and do not, get what they intend when
they paint. Yet the assertion holds if one sees that artists'
programs, wants, and intentions are themselves resultants

of various vectors, incorporations, and resolutions of com-
patible and conflicting factors. Thus when an artist thinks,
"I want to make such-and-such," this particular vision or
program is at the outset reflective of the possibilities of
paint *and* reflective of aesthetic beliefs *and* his psychic
needs *and* his hopes for art's future path, and so on; it
seems a single, a unitary intention but it is representative
of many forces.

Also, to speak of intentions as either fulfilled or not, and
beliefs about art as lived up to or not, misses the remark-
able operational effects of these factors in the creative
situation. To believe, for example, in Realism is to plant a
(only one) foot in a position; though one's other limbs
may be dancing wildly (one cannot legislate away his,
say, libidinous urges), they cannot dance too far from the
planted foot or the body breaks. So the work of this
believer (see Plate 15) is not a straight reflection of Realist belief but the belief establishes one end of a polarity,
giving his work a locus in the art realm and a particular
thrust, and also setting up a tension, say, between the cool
toughness of Realism and the warmer tendency to emotionalism, a tension which itself helps make the work
exciting. A similar effect is seen when the aim is a formal
one. Achievement of, say, depth is not minimal for success
for a painter seeking three-dimensional space, for a canvas
inevitably remains in fact flat and one cannot really succeed in gaining depth. But this aim sets up an interplay
between depth-suggesting devices and the canvas's un-
varying flatness, a tug-of-war which would not obtain
without this intention, being an intriguing good which
may make the painting succeed though the intention is
not fulfilled and is not fulfillable. Perhaps factional de-
bates among artists over partisan beliefs seem so pointless
because the factual rightness or wrongness of a belief

(e.g., The world needs flatness, or Realism, in art) seems secondary to the effect on one's work of choosing this or that position or of rationalizing one's proclivities thusly, secondary to the effect, in one's creative system-of-forces, of shooting a vector in this or that direction.

ART AND TIME

Now it may be objected that the model of creative behavior rendered above is more akin to a still photograph than a motion picture: duration is missing; contemporaneous and sequential relationships among instances of creative conduct is missing. Nowhere is the force, in creative situations, of the artists's awareness of such relationships depicted. I will soon comment on these relationships. However, the greatest objection will be to my depiction of the art enterprise as perhaps seething but not going anywhere. It will be asked, "But do not artists strive to make the concepts and methods of art grow? Is not art identifiable with an army ("avant-garde" being a metaphor drawn from military life) pushing ahead; are not only those in the vanguard heroes; is not this where artists should strive to be?

Resident in these questions is the very influential view of time as a stream in which humanity swims, forming a flow which pushes back human horizons. Man's consciousness is seen as ever unfolding, and art, especially pioneering art, shares in fostering this unfoldment. Now, the problem in challenging such influential views of history (and the art value system they foster) is that they make history. That is, they produce their own corroboration, in two ways: (1) by shaping our comprehension of the past, and (2) by shaping current and future events, inducing accordance of these with the perspective of the historian.

In respect to the past, the art histories men write obviously are not histories of everything that goes on in art; rather, one finds a record of selections comprising our histories, selections based upon some criteria of importance and value, chronicling only what was, in the historian's view, significant and worthwhile. But then this record becomes all the history most later men know of; it is the means by which the past is grasped. Furthermore, it determines the shape of the past in men's minds. Hence, to say, for example, that past art history *is* the story of art's onward and upward march is only to say that we have written histories of such marches and little else. Our books record emphatically those instances of art which are alignable in a progression; all others (e.g., instances of art's services to God or humanity, or non-progressive peaks of artistic excellence) are minimized. A census-like record of each and every useful occurrence in art may not buttress a view of art as a concerted effort to march forward. Our records, however, may express our western, Dionysian, progressionist criteria of selection and may give this support. Hence one holds suspect the corroboration of an influential view of art history by chronicles written by holders of this view, yet it is difficult to review the past intimately and reshape our conceptions of it, and challenge those prevalent views.

And an influential view of history shapes current and future history in that, for example, a belief in art as an advancing army acts as a force in creative situations and urges an artist to work in a manner he thinks is advanced, and as many men acquire and act upon this belief over time the history of art *becomes* the history of men taking up positions they consider in advance of those previously achieved. A leap-frog progression becomes occurrent: a force in current history difficult to challenge even though made real largely by belief in its past occurrence and inevitability.

The admonition to artists that they be in the vanguard is, then, difficult to oppose (and its reality as a current force impossible to deny). I will attempt this, however, by showing that the beliefs supporting this admonition are extremely flimsy. (Note that it is not vanguard works, artists, or their particular aesthetic concepts I oppose here, but the demand for a vanguardist stance.)

First, what might the notion of progress in art point to that might constitute its meaning and its thrust and tell men to participate in it? It is clear to all that one cannot go down through the ages from pre-history to the present and trace a rising level of aesthetic quality. The cave drawings at Altamira are as good as any made since, and such a lack of progress is, moreover, theoretically expecta-ble, for art performance ability is non-cumulative; each artist is a necessarily finite package of art skills, sensitivi-ties, experiences, etc. Some packages are large, some small, but expectably, succeeding ages do not make, in general, ever larger packages. If they are theoretically expandable it is so in the same (tiny) order of magnitude as, say, men's capacity to run the mile quickly. And as we have seen, art depends not upon accumulables (e.g., knowledge, power), which time provides to artists and might swell their capacities as generations passed, but rather upon organizations, marvels, relationships among givens, among some few selected things. And as soon as any few such things become available, they suffice to make possible unsurpassable art, such as was indeed created ages ago.

And dialectical growth is also impossible in art, for as we move from, say, soft-edge subjective painting (Plate 18) to hard-edge objective painting (Plate 4), we generally pay for the virtues of the latter by sacrificing the virtues of the former. And, as noted, even if one succeeds in synthesizing two or more sets of virtues, he then sacrifices the strength gained by standing in an uncompromised, extreme position, one whose toughness and singularity is attractive. So progress-believers would have no grounds for anticipation or assertion of progress as dialectical growth in aesthetic excellence. Neither in theory nor in practice can one find such grounds.

Nor may one assert that progress occurs, more generally, as growth in the human spirit, growth in which art participates. The potentials for human greatness may increase but so, too, do the potentials for human meanness, and everyone knows that both potentials are being, as ever, realized. All our journals reveal that as daily life becomes physically easier, the ease itself breeds boredom; as our purposes are ever more readily achieved we find life less challenging and unpleasantly lacking in purposiveness. More men than ever are governed by law, there are fewer barbarians, but corruption under law is as great as ever and the remaining barbarians make up by effectiveness for their lack of numbers. And it seems in the very nature of things that this be necessarily so, that, as it were, every new insecticide must prompt a strain of mosquitoes immune to it, that to be down is to want to go up; to be up is to find down one's only possibility; to be still is to become uncomfortably stiff. Each human spirit is potentially good and bad as ever. The thing called man does not grow, it squirms and copes, pleasantly or unpleasantly, well or poorly, with noble or base intentions, as one's case may be. Neither through art nor otherwise is there a general magnification of the human spirit, and though one can tell the artist that it is helpful when he scratches where he and his neighbors itch, one cannot admonish him to help with non-occurring growth.

But if the possibilities fulfillable in art are ever increasing is this not growth? Not of the excellence of individual painters and paintings or of humanity, but of the realm of art itself?

Theoretically this seems the case; if one lists the ways in which men may make art and make it serve them, the list is longer now than in, say, Rubens' day. However, the realm of art is primarily an existential, not a theoretical thing, consisting not of what in theory may be done but of people, things, and what *is* going on—and has the body of practice, products and phenomena *actually* grown? To point to my meaning: In the early years of our country, pioneers left behind thriving communities on our Atlantic Coast and in moving Westward and populating new territory, they increased the size of the American realm. But suppose instead *all* the residents of the Atlantic Seaboard shifted their homes Westward, leaving our Eastern states uninhabited and uncultivated. The American realm, then, might *in theory* extend from the Atlantic to, say, the Mississippi River, but if only the area between the Appalachians and the Mississippi were actually inhabited, the existential size of the realm would not have been increased by the migration. The realm, constant in size, would have merely shifted its locale. In art we have added in this century, for example, the things that Picasso and Pollock and Dada and Pop can do, but have not left behind thriving communities of Rembrandts, Rubens, or Michelangelos. So much of the land once inhabited has been left deserted and uncultivated, apparently unreclaimable, that to say that the realm is expanded seems less accurate than to say that it has shifted its locale without increasing its actual operative size. One's preference for Picasso over Rubens, or vice versa, is irrelevant here; the point is that a belief in progress cannot stand on the notion that progress consists in expanding the existential possibilities of art.

But here is the root of our trouble: men confuse progress in thinking *about* art with progress *in* art, confuse ideas with things. Certainly the range of attitudes in which the artist can work has increased and so have his ideas about what art can do, and with what it can do it. One surmises that Robert Rauschenberg *knows* more about art than Rubens knew. But this only assures that traffic in *ideas* is improving; art is increasingly *interesting—thought*-engaging. And with talk about art being ever extended geographically and socially, the coin of talk and ideas looms larger at times than actual art objects. Yet good and numerous ideas do not necessarily make better artists of the men who hold them, neither does a lack of ideas make bad artists. For (to repeat) an idea establishes a pole in a dualism; a painting will be, say, "this idea" *while* being very physical and sensuous. And this bipolarity *is* the marvel (affording delight) and not the quality of the idea pole itself. The "magic" is in the tension, not in the pulling agents. One who values ideas may be pleased to walk away from a painting with a (its) new idea—and a painting's illustration of a particular aesthetic position may help make the work interesting—but one can say *art* has progressed only if staying *with* the painting, long after the idea has done its provoking and improved one's thinking about art—and this is taken for granted—is better than staying with paintings of other eras. And this should occur consistently in one's experience. No one seriously claims this happens, and when we cease to confuse progress in *thinking* about art with progress *in* art, the latter progress will not be asserted.

And even if art were expandable in the sense in which our nation was expanded by pioneering Westward, this would not justify the vanguardist's inferences from or attitudes towards this fact. The men who expand art's possibilities deserve praise, but expansion of the realm of art itself is not the only service an artist may perform, nor is such service higher in an hierarchical order of importance than the other services art and artists perform. Yet vanguardists write, for example, of an artist whose work stems mainly from his continuing world-view and is not innovational as they would write of, say, Dr. Jonas Salk were he still repeating his work on the polio vaccine; that is, they imply either his senility, fear of moving from familiar ground, or inability or refusal to contribute further. They seem to base their allegations on the belief that in art as in pure science one is researching, innovating, or he is doing nothing. And while this may be true in science it is not true in art, for art proffers not concepts which once given are given for all men and are foolish to repeat, but *services* continuingly and recurrently needed, and which must be rendered to each individual when and as needed. The developer of innovations, then, serves in the art enterprise but in a way no more laudable or privileged theoretically than those who serve in other ways.

Neither are those artists who work in a manner that is being newly developed privileged, by their innovations, to place themselves above others who work in long-extant ways, nor to demonstrate, as the claim goes, that they know how art has changed and others do not. For after all a *new* possibility is just that and is *not* an obligation; it is a license one may be grateful for having but may or may not want to use. And while the realm of art after a new

development is different from the realm of art before this
development, it is different to the *extent* of the addition made, it is not *reformed* by the addition. There is a
new option in the seething system of forces constituting a
man's creative situation; but it does not, because new,
override other forces or reshape the dynamics of the situation or alter the artist's sense of what responsibility means
in it. If one's creative situation demanded before 1900
that he "ground" himself, send roots into and tie up with
the physical world, via visual realism (see Plate 12)—and
this demand, not the audience's need or lack of need for
likenesses is usually what drives realists—that was the job
of this artist then *and after* the development of abstraction. After 1900, Realism *was* not his only available possibility but it *is* his privilege always. And his continuance as
Realist does not imply his failure to see how the job of the
artist has changed, for this job remains the growing of the
sorts of things described herein through living in accordance with the forces in his situation.

All of which is to say that whatever growth the realm of
art may undergo does not justify the vanguardist's inferences therefrom about what this growth says to and about
artists; indeed, neither this growth nor any other tells the
artist to allow "pioneering" concerns to influence him at
all.

Now it might seem that an emphasis on vanguardism is
beneficial in that at least it is against academicism. That
is, since many painters, unfortunately, produce canvases
by a routine method, vanguard beliefs, it might seem,
would be helpful in urging one not to be such a stick-
in-the-mud but to be up there facing the challenges in
one's situation. This would be fine if it did not posit a
choice only between working in one's routine method and
working at some stylistic frontier. For in fact a third possi-

bility exists, that of letting one's work emerge afresh each day out of a continuing struggle with one's questions, one's life, one's talents, whether what emerges resembles other work or is exploratory. In its positing a choice of stance between two possibilities, instead of including that other one in which integrity lies, even the anti-academic thrust of the army-progress position is weakened.

Also weakening its anti-academic thrust is the fact that, although it seems theoretically possible to say that some artistic directions and styles have more pertinence and value to art and one's time than others, and that one ought to work at such, there can be no counterpart in the artist's reality to such an assertion; it is incongruent with anything he can experience; it says nothing he can profitably listen to. If the present era is marked by tension, danger, neuroticism, should one, pursuant to vanguard beliefs, face and reflect this fact—or in an harmonious, ordered art offer an alternative to it? At what frontier is one to serve? And if our culture is shabby, commercialized, banal, is it pioneering to simply admit it into art? To make the gesture of embracing nothingness? Or aestheticize it? Satirize it? Make it a pole in a fine arts–commercial art dualism? Or not to add to the existant shabbiness more of the same? A tenable case can be made in defense of calling any of these choices "up front." And when Stuart Davis made an abstraction of a cigarette package (plate 24), how should he then, were he given prescience, or now define it pursuant to vanguard beliefs? As rear guard abstraction (it did not go nearly so far in abstraction as paintings by Kandinsky and Picasso already had)? Or as an avant-garde scouting foray for Pop Art? The painting cannot be ranked in such terms at all, least of all by the artist. And would he not follow his ingrained life style, his way, irrespective of this consideration? All of which is to

24. Stuart Davis, *Lucky Strike* (1921). In 1921: conservative abstraction—or a bold advance toward Pop Art? (Collection, The Museum
of Modern Art, New York. Gift of the American Tobacco Company,
Inc. Photographed for the Museum by Soichi Sunami)

say that the belief that the needs of one's times, or one's task in a march, privilege some art approaches over others is without possible existential counterpart in, relevence to, or accordance with the artist's daily life. The admonition to be avant-garde rests on unexamined and flimsy notions, historical happenstance, points nowhere, and is well ignored by artists.

Now it may be objected that there must be *some* foundation for the widespread belief that a man's art should reflect his times, even though one searches in vain for a good argument yielding this "should" as a conclusion. This muddle arises because it has been easy to argue not that one's art *should* but rather that it indeed *does* reflect his times (although often indirectly); we have failed to see the different implications for artistic conduct between the admonition and the proposition. The "should" points to an obligation, requiring our attention, while if art *does* in fact reflect the times one can go his way without concern in this regard, *assuming* that *whatever* his choices his time and place in the world will have had a role in shaping them. When we cease to confuse a description of what occurs naturally with an obligation to attend to contemporaneity, then we will be free of this muddle.

If one must have a physical metaphor to point quickly to how artists' situations exist among those surrounding them in space and time, I would first picture each artist as jumping as high as he can from his ground, his human needs, environs, talents, heritage, etc. Of course artists do see and are influenced by each other, and so one may get a boost up from a neighbor or ancestor in space or time, or he may mimic him, or his neighbor's leap may spark his own to new though different heights. The ground in some places and some times may be better for aesthetic jumping than others, more nourishing to the jumper, more rewarding of his efforts, or simply less comfortable to remain earthbound on. One may leap in unison or in league with others or alone. The changing forces operative in each creative situation yield fresh leaps each day. Bravery consists of commitment to this process, however unpredictable and however dangerous, or safe, it is; it does not entail purposely trying, or avoiding, new gyrations in new places periodically. Some original leaps by new figures will be seen occasionally. They are not *ipso facto* higher than those of other men. One welcomes and might be effected by them to the extent of their height and for whatever goods they yield, and for the interesting change they afford. One does not think that their newness makes them overwhelmingly laudable or that it necessarily changes the nature of the art enterprise and domain. And the differing sorts of ground in the realm, those marked by emotionalism, naturalism, idealism, etc., remain continuingly or at least recurrently springy; to make a grand leap, one need not ignore one's natural homestead or meandering path and troop to the grounds where others are pitching their tents and are leaping well, nor take on a task in common with them. (See Plates 25, 26.) Indeed, the citizenry of the realm does not as a body move in concert; it is not a nation-as-a-whole on the march; it is too variegated for that. Out of the individual jumping comes goods of various sorts, for the jumper, for his comrades in art, and for the larger domain of human life. As stated before, men's aspirations are crystallized, their wishes are realized for imagination to hold, their feelings are articulated and ordered, possibilities are made contemplatable, their environs are made clearer, and so on. The realm is not going anywhere; it is a place for and way of living. This is enough.

25. Velásquez, *Camillo Astalli, Cardinal Pamphili.* (See Plate 26.)
(Hispanic Society of America)

26. Robert La Hotan, *Meadow with Tree* (1965). If art is in the marvels, and if the ground of art remains springy everywhere, why not this, too? (See also Plate 25.) (Courtesy of the artist, photographed by Walter Rosenblum)

3

Art and Audience

THE MODE OF THOUGHT SUGGESTED ABOVE MAY HELP ONE understand some aspects of art and audience relationships. And currently these relationships are badly misunderstood.

For example, the audience is often blindly egocentric in that it assumes that it is being confronted with Painting A because its maker thought it an especially good idea to present such to *them*. Their gratification is what art is for, of course. Often if the work seems irrelevant to its desires, the audience cannot even imagine why it was produced. The audience does not understand that the artist may act as he does, not in order to provide a spectacle the audience desires, but because his act and its yield seems inevitable or desirable to the artist. (Plate 27.) This is not a matter of self-coddling or therapy, either. Edward Hopper, for instance, would instruct and entertain his audience more if, over his long career, he changed his style occasionally, put a new act on stage, as it were, but appar-

27. Ralph Ortiz, *Archaeological Find, 3* (1961). The art act (here "destructive"), a way of living for the artist, and, as gesture, significant to the audience. (Collection, The Museum of Modern Art, New York. Gift of Mrs. Constance Levene. Photographed by Eric Pollitzer)

ently his vision is one with the man and is consistent and he cannot and should not put a new face on the world when he cannot truthfully say he finds one there. (See Plate 28.) Not therapy but one's own onwardness and integrity may necessitate one's acting without notice of the audience.

On the other hand, the artist is often blindly egocentric in that he fails to see that he is not acting for himself alone. He does, after all, proffer his work to others, in the presumption that some value will be found in it by some in the audience. He may assume that he can give this value best by following his own bent and not watching the audience, not jumping off-stage to see how he looks to others, for service need not depend upon desire or intention to serve, but the artist does make the assumption that his work has some social as well as personal worth.

It seems sensible, then, for each to play their role, not switch them around, but for each to cognize what the other's role involves. The artist cannot ask that the audience appreciate what he does because it gratifies *him;* the members of the audience cannot ask that the artist ignore his needs to gratify *them.* Each looks to the creative act and object for something else, but can look at each other with respect for what they are doing (if indeed they act, each from his own standpoint in a way worthy of respect).

But if their needs and aims differ, how do artist and audience meet each other?

As noted, the creative act is *as such* important to the artist. And, when it is known to the audience, it may be important to it as a symbolic gesture. But to both the object is very important. The artist acting does so *towards* an object; he may love the dancing but he also keeps an

28. Edward Hopper, *Nighthawks* (1942). Painting giving continuing services, which, unlike giving concepts, cannot be made pointless through repetition. (Courtesy of The Art Institute of Chicago, Friends of American Art Collection)

eye on how "the dance" is turning out. And for members of the audience, since the act is usually unknown to them, the object is clearly the more important. In any case, the object is, as it were, the end (yield) of the artist's art experience and the object is the beginning of the audience's; where the artist bids a painting goodbye the audience bids it hello. The object is, then, their meeting ground.

How good is it as such? Because this art making and taking procedure would seem an interpersonal act if the object acted as mediator, it has seemed nice to think of the whole affair as akin to a person leaving a helpful friendly note or other sort of communication to others whom he cannot otherwise contact or cannot tell what he will without such notes. Yet we have observed that, in fact, the art object is a thing, and while some such things *express*, not all do appreciably and none do *only* that. That is, unlike a personal note, the art object is, in being a thing, an item of many potentials, limited in number but having many still when compared to those of, say, a statement. And to this thing must come a variety of viewers and, as noted before, each one may be theoretically capable of realizing only any one or two, or all, or none of these potentials. Also, the object is generated by a complex system of forces, not a single aim. Due, then, to the impossibility of a work being shaped only by an aim, and due to the manyness of its potentials, art objects are not, and could not be made, so as to assure (or preclude) comprehension by others, or approval. Nor could they be made to fulfill the very different complexes of needs respective viewers bring to paintings. The object, then, is not simply a means of communication between artist and audience. It is not satisfactory as an interpersonal meeting ground.

However, the object is, we noted, the artist's provision of company for the audience. And if the object is gratifying company for a viewer we may say that that viewer is one of the artist's spiritual brothers. The artist assumes and anticipates that some such exist, that some, as it were, resonate on his frequency. He also assumes many are no kin to him at all. These assumptions entail no respect or disrespect for "the public," but say rather that "the public"—even the art or expert public—is a fiction; there is only a potential fraternity around each work of art, composed of he who made it as he found he had to and those who find being with it good. (Admittedly, knowledge of this situation encourages an attitude of cosy privatism among some artists, the relishing of favor among and services to a small coterie of friends; but, of course, the notion of art's potential universality encourages the tendency to measure an artist as one does a movie star, by box office appeal or ability to act as love-object for the greatest number of people, and this too is unfortunate.) For better or worse, art's services are necessarily selective and limited ones. To those who find a work gratifying a service is rendered, and to the extent that a good is achieved, society is benefited. If our philosophies are at all sound, the art enterprise as a whole materializes and makes contemplatable men's wishes, aspirations, irritations, feelings, and enables catharsis, psychic growth, etc.; in doing so, for many men, it objectifies the soul-state and fosters the movements of our time. But this does not say each (or even a great) work of art has such grand capacities. A work of art is a universal only in the sense that men of different nations, places, cultures, and eras may constitute the fraternity around it; it transcends boundaries, but not in the sense that it can potentially serve every man. A work of art is theoretically, as well as in practice, limited to going from a man to some men; and only in serving the part can it serve Man.

But beyond the relationships cited above as obtaining among art and human needs, there is one other I would like to specify. To understand it is to understand why art and society are currently locked in an ambivalent marriage, wherein love and hate are not only present and often indistinguishable but are each necessary for the marriage to endure, much as in some romantic couplings.

Let me try to point to this relationship indirectly at first: One may say that there are several ways in which death gives meaning to life. Most of us probably do not believe that it is one's inevitable dying which makes the living of his life worthwhile—it is not in this respect that death gives meaning to life—but certainly the concept "alive," that which has life, would be meaningless without the concept "dead," lifeless. For if all existent things were alive, and never to be otherwise, we would never have the concept as a meaningful one; it is our awareness of the contrast of these two categories of existence— each to the other—that gives rise to distinguishing and distinctive concepts of them. This awareness of contrast is the source of one's meanings; for their meanings they are thusly interdependent.

And this interdependence operates even in the matter of our feelings about living. Although even an animal may, speaking loosely, enjoy living, and although rarely does the thought of our eventual demise enhance our days, still the feeling of being alive is made a treasured one, one appreciated and not taken for granted, by contrast with the other well-known possibility. This is often noted by men who return to daily living after being close to dying. So the idea that something can be made meaningful and especially valued by its conspicuous contrast with what it is *not,* is readily admissible.

And in this vein of thought it is not unreasonable to ask, "By contrast with what is the concept "art" made meaningful and valuable?" Let us consider a behavioral aspect of art: art-creative conduct. To clarify the question: if all behavior were artistic we could speak only of human conduct and have no such concept as artistic conduct. But, I am suggesting, we do have this concept and have it because some behavior exists which is different from art conduct. Hence we ask, "What is this different-from-artistic sort of behavior which sets art into contrast?"

A clue to our answer lies in the fact that, in the realm we discuss, the art–nature difference is the one most often honored. Earlier we noted that to loom as an art object an item must seem given by man-as-artist rather than by nature's forces. But the art–nature differentiation gives meaning and value to art by opposition, and in the way indicated above, only if we contrast not simply man's art conduct with "nature" in the sense of the operations of wind and sea, nor also with "nature," as shown in man's animal-like behavior. For the latter is not the natural in contemporary human life. The life that is natural to men today is that of the acculturated person living in a societal context. It is civilized life, at whatever the level. Certainly this is natural in that commonly it is this against which deviations, the unnatural, are measured; we know that a man is not said to behave "naturally" when he acts like a beast but when he behaves as his culture expects. And, I suggest, it is by contrast with man's natural behavior as acculturated citizen that his behavior as artist, in this respect the unnatural, becomes distinctive; it is this contrast that gives meaning and especial value to the contrasting types.

Because some men glibly say that art mirrors its cultural context or that it rebels against it, let me try to say clearly the major way in which it seems to me this artistic-behavior–cultural-behavior contrast obtains.

In *Psychotherapy, East and West*[1] Alan Watts points out that according to field theory in psychology a man is an organism who structures his world and also *is* structured not only by his physical environment but by his conceptual structuring of it. This indicates that organism and environment are not separate and discrete realities, but rather that man and world interpenetrate and give form each to the other. And in developing, a child gains a schema, a diagrammatic way of seeing things, and he sees and holds reality *in* this way. One's schema shapes one's grasp of his world and, insofar as his experience is concerned, reality is clay shaped by this grasp.

Futhermore, schematizing is not merely a temporal characteristic of contemporary men. Even if one cannot prove the point and can frame it only loosely, one seems warranted in saying that if a man lacking such a schema could be placed in an environment in no way structured on the face of it or by other men, he would construct a framework into which his sensations could be placed and ordered. This is to say that for whatever causes and reasons, whether through evolution, divine gift, historical happenstance, the intrinsic qualities of the species or otherwise, humans now have the propensity to be structurers of their environs; they are inveterate schematizers.

Indeed, a creature who lacked this propensity, who could not and would not even try to "make sense of things," would seem not really human, despite his manlike form. And this is one reason why the fancied situation of the schematically unequipped man in the unstructured environment is only loose talk; that is, "schematically une-

quipped *man*" is a contradiction within itself. The other
reason is that such a creature is an unrealizable fiction;
nobody in fact grows from childhood into manhood without being instructed in how to see things, in schematizing.
One's culture, through its language, mores, religion, formal and informal tutors, familial and societal structure,
etc. gives the growing child the framework into which the
datum of experience is organized, indeed through which
it is filtered and *becomes* experience. And the depth and
breadth of this process must be clear if art's function is to
be seen. One is taught not merely "how to behave properly" by the culture's laws and customs, but one is given a
particular grasp of reality, i.e., his culture's, and this incul-
cation of a principle of configuring reality has the strong-
est effect of acculturation upon the person. When Watts
says that growing up and becoming acculturated is in
effect "learning to play the game" he can be interpreted as
meaning this almost literally. That is, the child is given
not a fresh world, a boundless unorganized meadow
which he is to make sense of, but a *field* laid out by his
culture, which like a ball field has its bounds drawn, its
foul lines established, proper positions defined, the meaning of play articulated, etc. And much as the ball field
is the world of the game participant, the field as structured by the culture is eventually the reality, and the only
reality, the child sees. His non-schematic or unacceptable
schematic ways of structuring are suppressed (which may
be one reason why early childhood experience cannot be
remembered). He learns not merely to conform but to
form in a special way. The adult, then, in that he has a
schematizing procedure and sees an "organized" reality,
does not have the opportunity to go, as it were, as an untutored innocent into an unstructured "meadow" and
make a field of it afresh.

But we know that often there are reasons why this opportunity is desired. Sometimes the culture's schematizing procedure is one unprofitable for the culture as a whole or some group of its members. For example, the culture which thinks in terms of animism and magic may therefore be damaged recurrently by nature or by its efficient scientific neighbor. On the other hand, in the scientific culture some people's need for the magical and the numinous may be painfully thwarted. Individuals may, then, wish for the fresh chance, that of the innocent in an unstructured world, for collective or personal reasons.

But also there is a more general, pervasive, and fundamental reason for this desire. It is the wish to be out from under the compulsory, the ought-to-be, the necessary. Whether what *must be* according to one's culture seems right to one or not, and whether it is rewarding or not, its sheer must-ness is oppressive. One may wish the fresh chance, then, not only to get a particular something one wants, but to just feel its freshness, to be free of the bonds of responsibility to ordinary necessities.

But how to get the fresh chance?

To get satisfactions not realizable in one's own culture one can, conceivably, emigrate and gain the world view of another culture, one in which personal satisfaction is attainable. But the new culture will have *its* world view and hence its oppressiveness, too. (Even bohemia is *insistent* upon freedom and irresponsibility, and by making these mandatory robs them of their freshness.) Even if one is sufficiently independent and brilliant to schematize the world all anew, if he does so according to his best lights, in seeking rightness and in apparently finding it he would find obligations, necessitation, and oppression. He would still be in the world of seriousness, the world of work. Hence Watts interprets Zen as recommending not that one literally quit his culture and world-view but "see through it." By seeing that his world-view, inherited or self-originated, is not *the* reality principle but *one way* of schematizing the world, its oppressiveness is relieved. One decides, perhaps, to play his culture's game but by taking it *as* a game, his feeling that he *must* live, and must live in thus-and-so a manner, is transformed into "just living"; i.e., playing the position, arguing with the umpire, accepting the givenness of the givens, *as in a game* and no more seriously.

The problem with Watts' view is that while one's ethics, metaphysics, religion, and ontology may not say that one *must* live, in practice the desire of most men to go on living, however derived, provides a "must" that is the equivalent in their lives of theoretic mandates. "To live, to die" cannot be said to equal "To play, to cease playing." And the desire of most men for survival makes the formation of a profitable reality schema a very serious affair and not a game-like matter. Also, it is serious for those men who cannot be sane without *trying* to have their thoughts accord with the objective world, even if trying is futile and such accordance is a meaningless notion. For to not care about the right and true in areas where they matter seems merely perverse, senseless, even insane. . . .

Also, Watts fails to grant the gratifying advantages of seriousness as a life posture. For to posit a venture as serious sometimes causes tension and pain, but also one often reduces pleasure as well as pain by not taking one's situations seriously; to not really try often conduces to less fun, in games and in life-at-large. It seems, then, that we have need of the serious, work-like posture, and while it may do no good to overlay such needs with theoretic compulsion, it seems impossible and undesirable for most men to be game-like in life and *thusly* get out from under culture's tendency to impose mandates.

But this is what games—and art—are for. To put it loosely, there is no need to be playful at work, when there is, contrived to this end, a place for playfulness: games, art. But because an identification of play and art has so often been libelously made, and "play" so ill-defined, let me put the matter clearly:

To construct a game is to take a batch of space and time and to structure it, freshly (and structure men must), as one would have it, as a world or system one can live in for a while. But a game is a construct which its maker knows need not be inevitably or lastingly *as* it is—the rules could have been otherwise and can be altered, and so too for the field itself. And moreover it need not *be* at all, it is gratuitous. In making and participating in a game one thusly lives outside all the "musts" except those of one's own adoption. And even the basis for adoption is not necessarily one's best estimation of truth or goodness or something otherwise obligatory. One chooses, apparently at least, unnecessarily, arbitrarily, gratuitously, without responsibility to one's own or another's normal every-day standards (only the demands of attention need be met and the "logic" of the construction procedure fulfilled), and this is what we *mean by action in "the spirit of play."* And living occasionally in this spirit seems a sensible alternative to on the one hand never structuring the world afresh and never escaping the mandatory, and on the other hand being, perversely, always playful, even in grave everyday situations. So it seems that games are wanted for the fulfillment of specific needs, e.g., to exercise mind and muscle, to cooperate and compete with others, to vent aggressiveness; but they are also desired for living in *their* spirit, wherein one comes out from under the musts of one's culture and other seriously designed schemas.

In some of these respects art and games are alike. As in game construction, in art too the feeling of being out from under prevails; one has the chance as an adult to enter with the stance of the innocent into an unstructured world, and to structure it as a world for attention to live in for a while. And this is desired in part because specific goods can be achieved thusly, e.g., wishes fulfilled, visions crystallized, but also because the sheer feeling of the freshness of one's opportunity, the gratuitousness and freedom of it all, is desired, irrespective of specific goods achieved.

Yet, despite similarities, the differences between art and games also must be honored. Anyone who notes that mankind has constructed games throughout history and devotes tremendous thought, time, and energy to them, would not say that because their dynamics are described as playful and, vis-à-vis culture, non-serious they serve no serious function in life. Rather, one concludes that man has a serious need to be playful at times and hence a need for a context wherein non-seriousness seems appropriate, i.e., the game context. But in art the seriousness of men's needs for it is manifested in the seriousness of art's surface. Even the sportive and amusing does not loom as "fooling around," and when Clive Bell writes of art's least common denominator as "significant form" he is symptomizing men's impression that art indeed seems to exhibit significance, in the sense of bearing both import and importance. We come to art "in the spirit of play," out from under the culture's schemas and our own usual standards, but we play not with sticks, balls, markers—implements with no inherent or intrinsic meanings or with meanings arbitrarily assigned to them. We "play" with that which *matters* on the face of it, if not literally and in the frame of thinking of our culture, then in our feelings about them, in our intuition of them. When one wants to be carefree he turns to games; art is where one goes to "play" with what he cares about and as an innocent in a world that is yet to be made.

It may be clear, then, how art creative conduct contrasts with acculturated conduct. Art behavioral dynamics and its reasons for being make art conduct at least theoretically *irrespective* of culture; art behavior is a-cultural as a mode of conduct—but I rush to say that this is not a contrast between antagonists *or* dissimilar friends. In art, the culture's ways of schematizing and its ideas are held, theoretically, as irrelevant; one is to start afresh. In being a-cultural, art is not necessarily being simply a mirror of culture or necessarily a critic of it, but is sometimes one, sometimes the other, and sometimes is linked to culture in still more intricate and interesting ways. Acting irrespective of culture the artist may purport to give new and outlandish "answers"—but, he finds belatedly and sadly, to questions his culture posed. Or he may reject these questions in favor of others, playing a new game as it were, only to find that his culture's questions and the acts of rejecting them determined *what* others he was to take up. And even when in an innocent's posture (it is never a really innocent man who takes art's fresh chance), the artist is not an untutored infant. So the artist may make, as we hear, a new and more intense world, or a more ordered one, and sometimes he indeed sees afresh; but at other times the intensity and order may be demanded by the lack of these in the everyday world, or demanded by a personality shaped in the world. Thusly the culture-life is usually still a major force even in creative situations which in principle stand aside from culture and wherein cultural traits are not directly reflected. We have, then, the artist standing irrespective of culture, but it is the life in and of culture that gives him the need to so stand and influences what he does in this stance.

Thusly, art and culture stand locked together but in a peculiar way. Art is *valued* partly because in its posture it is aside from cultural patterns, but art finds culture-patterns essential to its meaning and functioning—as something to be aside from. Art's arbitrariness, irresponsibility, playfulness, *is* such only *vis à vis* culture; it is, as noted, apparently logical and necessitated within itself. Hence art requires culture to seem lawful, serious, staid, and thusly maintain contrast. Like male and female, art–culture differences alienate while they bind, and give meaning to each other's gender.

And the community's feelings about art reflect the ambivalence of their relationship. Art objects usually loom to their audience as beautiful, pleasure-giving and highly desirable. But one must often stand open to a new world schema to realize art's pleasure-giving potential, and this is upsetting. Also, the artist as a man may be no better or worse and no more or less wise than other men, but in his freedom to be a-cultural he seems both admirable and dangerous; he cannot be anticipated as can those men who "play the game" we all know. Great artists are classified as being among a culture's treasures, but so are bright children, caged tigers, and saints—and they are, still, not comforting to be with. Civilization needs the artist's unconcern for civilization's schemas for play and to preview new ways of seeing, but it is not happy to *have* the need of this attitude. Yet ambivalence, the very tension, is healthful and necessary if art and audience are to serve each other best. Were art and culture to be fully amalgamated, they would eliminate, with respect to each other, their reasons for being (See Plates 29, 30.) Admittedly there has always been amalgamated establishment art, academic art—art which, as it were, tried personal play in a well-accepted game—but there has also always been, with-in such art and outside it, a component which saw the world afresh, and thereby earned praise *and* damnation. So be it.

29. Morris Graves, *Little Known Bird of the Inner Eye* (1941). To amalgamate art's way with culture's way is to lose the contrast that makes art valuable. (Collection, The Museum of Modern Art, New York. Purchase. Photographed for the Museum by Soichi Sunami)

30. Jack Levine, *Welcome Home*. (See Plate 31.) (Courtesy of the Brooklyn Museum)

4

The Education of the Painter in Painting

I DO NOT ATTEMPT TO PRESENT HERE A COMPREHENSIVE proposal for or description of the education of painters in their art. Rather, I try to respond to just a few questions of persistent interest in this area.

FREEDOM AND AIMS OF PAINTING EDUCATION

Prominent among persistent questions are these two: "What are painting students to learn?" and "How much freedom may they have while learning what they must?" I would like to suggest here that attainment of the freedom experienced by the artist is the chief objective of painting education, it is a goal and not a condition of it, and that students are to learn what they must to make them free, precisely as an artist is. Let us defer the second question as stated (with its use of "freedom" as "a range of options") and let us inquire into what the artist's freedom means and what is requisite for it.

Despite his sometime difficulties the artist experiences, as a professional, a feeling of freedom; it is one which, he may believe, privileges his vocation over others. Yet by objective measure, seen from without, he is not free. Rather, he is bound up by his commitments, predilections, urges, tastes, etc. He is not even free to exercise "the rights of artists," whatever these might be, since he is not "artists" but one in particular, with, say Smith's history, talents, interests, etc. He can exercise only his own possessions, or rather is exercised by them. He is a directed creature. But he feels free because he identifies his directors with himself—they are internalized if not originally internal. And because their value and necessity he respects, as he does that of "the truth," he feels he moves "on his own."

Moreover, without such directors he could not feel free. One recalls having leisure time when, if he feels directed by nothing, he feels not free but only restless and discontented. Indeed, even doing what one acknowledges as "good" things, if one has no active desire to do them, does not incite the feeling of freedom. Movement, in line with and generated by endorsable drives and necessities, is necessary for the feeling of freedom.

And this is also to say that the crystallization (and internalization) of desires, drives, commitments, so that they can indeed direct one (and actually or apparently from within) and not be just amorphous seethings, is necessary for the feeling of freedom. And in the artist this has occurred and continues to occur. And so, too, the *understanding* of aesthetic necessities *as* such is a requisite, understanding the artist has—whether intuitively or intellectually or both. And also necessary, in addition to the impulsion to move, is the ability to move. One experiences no feeling of freedom if one simply feels and endorses some particularized urges but is unable to actually undergo pursuit of them. The artist is able to move (though not always without difficulty).

The artist's conduct and condition, then, is one of being locked in a deterministic situation, some of which is constituted of forces he brings to the situation, some of impersonal sources internalized, a situation in which, metaphysically, he is not free, but in which he feels free, as he lives and moves in a oneness with these forces. His freedom is an aspect of the creative phenomena sketched in the previous chapter.

Now, schools can grant or refuse its students options (e.g., to attend class or not as they please, to paint as they will, or to pursue assigned problems) but they cannot grant freedom. As described here freedom is an aspect of the conduct and condition of the *artist*. And if the student can display this conduct and condition upon simply being allowed to by his instructors, he is an artist already and not a student (except in the broad sense that all artists continue to study) and the school did not grant his freedom but only tolerated its exercise. And if the student is indeed such, a neophyte, he has little of value when his school acts as if it could grant him freedom; presumably he can gain the absence of annoyance, the only value in such granting, by painting at home. It may now be clear, therefore, why I am urging that schools consider, instead of granting or refusing to grant it, enabling freedom; that they take as their goals the achievement of whatever abilities are requisite for the artist's free condition.

Now we can infer what these abilities are from the description of freedom rendered here, but we would find that the inferences coincide with the abilities students have generally achieved heretofore as they became artists. Let me be descriptive of such actual achievement, then, from knowledge of art education, and artists' development, rather than prescriptive from theoretic inference. And let the coincidence of what my reflections would prescribe and what actually occurs indicate that the chief aim of painters' education not only ought to be but has been in effect if not in theory, the achievement of freedom (and, of course, the acts and objects of which it is an aspect). And let me indicate *how* this is fulfilled by the learnings attained.

STRANDS OF LEARNING

What constitutes the learning the painter achieves as he moves from beginning student to practicing artist?

The learnings generally have several intertwined strands of change characterizing them.

Perhaps most obvious among them is the change (soon to be examined further) from ineptitude to skillfulness, from clumsiness to know-how.

And only slightly less conspicuous is the change in students from limiting and inhibiting naïve conceptions of art to more sophisticated ones as they approach "understanding." For example, students move from considering the canvas simply as a ground *on* which one is to paint objects or shapes to considering the making of a painting as an entirety *of* the canvas, the latter evidencing perhaps objects and shapes but not acting simply as a platform for such. And from thinking of "how-to-paint-heads" and "these-colors-I-like" they move to thinking of what seems aesthetically called for and right, and of organization and of the process of painting. They cease to identify either speed of execution or painstaking care with naturalness, which sometimes calls for deliberation, sometimes for the spontaneous gesture. And they move from a concern with inspiration and talent to a concern with increasing their formal sensitivity and powers of imagination and drafts-manship, as it becomes clear that while the former are real and important matters, attention to them is less fruitful than attention to the latter. And, in the student's life, art is seen as less an opportunity for fun or therapy or bohem-ianism or rebellion and more a profession or calling, wherein great things can be done and wherein one can be a man-in-the-world in a good way. And the neophyte's view of art's history and its current ways broadens and deepens, as one sees, for example, the grounds from which different men have leaped, the differences among world view as well as among, say, color-usages, that are evi-denced in different art movements. Growth in under-standing of art, though variously comprised, is always conspicuous in the neophyte's development into artist-hood.

But not only has growth in skills and understanding characterized the development of artists *de facto;* such development is in theory a requisite for the feeling of freedom. For every situation (even in so plastic a realm as art) is a morass in which one cannot move and hence cannot feel free to the person who is inept and ignorant. Anyone who has tried without know-how to move in a desired painterly direction experiences ensnarement, not freedom. On the other hand, the skillful, informed man feels free in many a difficult situation because his potency makes him an overriding force and because the unmov-able may seem transparent, perhaps rightfully necessary, and hence less oppressively constraining.

Also, skills and knowledge open vistas and paths, in-creasing the feeling of freedom by granting, even prior to desire, the liberty inherent in a great number of choices available to one. And, on the negative side, after enough abortive efforts, one may even envision only as far as the limits of one's potentialities for realization of his visions. So skills and understanding are needed in respect to freedom for what they allow and what they do not preclude: openness to possibilities. (See Plate 31.) And it is for these reasons they characterize the development of artists.

This begs the question of *what* skills are requisites. Teachers usually infer these from their knowledge and experience of the art enterprise, fostering those which are apparently recurrently useful to artists. I would only stress here that while one cannot choose to teach every skill artists ever developed, the greater the number, the greater the choice of path—and the greater the freedom that eventually becomes available to the painter.

Also, if the several sorts of grounds from which artists leap are continuingly or even recurringly springy, then no skills become obsolete. If, say, the human being is sometimes and by some artists to be averted in favor of an alternative creature, and sometimes and by some men to be confronted or referred to directly, with the possibility of art production always present in these aversions *and* in these confrontations, then the skills needed, to both take and leave the human figure, may well be learned. However, my specific emphases are less important than my insistence that a decision on what skills to learn be made by each art educator, that they not be ignored or minimized lest freedom and creativity be thusly made impossible. One is, I am saying, to foster understanding and skills not in sad necessity but to enable freedom.

But the ability to move as the artist does and to feel free requires more of one than the assets cited this far. And so among the strands of learning in an artist's development

31. Daumier, *Conseil de Guerre.* Freedom is impossible, lacking the
capacities for moving with one's choices. (See also Plate 30.)
(Metropolitan Museum of Art, Schiff Fund, 1922)

there is also occurrent the growth in his ability to work in an artist's posture, to be active and responsive and think- ing *as* an artist is, and not otherwise. This development has several subtle aspects. For example, in my phenome- nological sketch I noted that the artist follows inclinations and visions the justification of which he may not know; and he moves in response to intuitions of what "feels" right; and, it seems, drives overt and covert, lofty and base, merge naturally in his behavior; and yet- to-be-realized projections of his imagination appear at least as worthy to him as analyses of the already existent. Intellect and reason, then, are not his chief measure of what is good, true, and real. And if a membrane exists between his conscious and unconscious minds it is pene- trable enough to allow free confluence of impulses from both into directives for behavior. And he dares to launch himself into the yet-to-be, the future, without a map, either because he is courageous, or he is forcefully im- pelled despite his fears, or he trusts his navigational apparatus no matter what may appear. Also, if he lets his actions and answers emerge afresh each day out of contin- uing struggle with himself, his questions, and his environ- ment, he lives endlessly with uncertainty and he often sees himself and the world in a deeper and possibly more painful way than he would were he to stand less openly. The artist is generally able to face this uncertainty and the seeing of the unpleasant. Now the psychic alignment, the stance, involved in these abilities and behavior patterns, while not reserved for artists alone, differs from that of most men as they stand in the world, including that of beginners in painting. Hence, growth in the capacity to stand as an artist does rather than in the stance of the neophyte is another major strand in his development.

Indeed, were one needlessly inhibited, closed, afraid to

move without certainty, his feeling free in art would be impossible. One need not be a paragon of mental health to be an artist; one need be able to work in the stance described, and therein feel free.

And these technical, conceptual, and psychological growth strands, while not identical with each other, are greatly interdependent. A student's apparent lack of, say, good color judgment may not be simply that but perhaps a failure to respond to his good perception of what is called for, out of fear of doing something he cannot intellectually justify beforehand. And many students suddenly show an apparent increase in skills when skills are not really increased but are only released by new faith in their intuitions, faith fostered by a sound understanding of art. On the other hand, as skills are developed, otherwise unconfident students, feeling their newfound potency gain confidence (and may then beneficially give vent also to their intuitive powers). And, of course, influencing all these aspects of development are the strengths, weaknesses, and events of one's daily personal life. So, growth along one strand of development abets that along another, or its lack retards other growth, and each is divorceable from the others only in words, not in actuality.

An additional strand of growth is necessary for maximal experiencing of the feeling of freedom, and that is change from the neophyte's pattern of flitting erratically from this and that approach, wherein nothing is integral with him, to the artist's finding (at least tentatively) what is usually if imprecisely called his "style." Admittedly, in current practice styles often become only frozen trademarks of artists, and style development is often narrowly conceived, arbitrarily and for bad reasons demanded, and at too early an age. Yet this development is, when genuine, a part of maturation and is necessary because it involves the crystallization of desires, commitments, wants, cited before as requisite for feeling free.

To convey the development's meaning more fully, let us consider a problem: one would think that two sides of a theoretic coin would make style-development difficult. On the one side, it seems terrifying to make choices when, to use Camus' phrase, everything is permitted and nothing is authorized. On the other side, partisans claiming authority status are always arguing that this or that style is theoretically privileged, stating cases which are, however, no more convincing than those of other advocates. How, then, does an artist choose his way when there are no guiding arrows, or only untrustworthy ones pointing everywhere? It seems impossible.

The artist does move, of course, but not because he chooses a direction. Rather it is because the operation of a system of forces rejects the irresolvable tangle of everything-is-permitted, nothing-is-authorized and *yields* (does not decide upon) action. All the forces in one's situation and not only one's beliefs on partisan or philosophic cases, determine one's direction. One has a resultant, not a conclusion, and this privileges one direction over another—in fact, not in theory—in that one's necessity seems privileged. This resultant accounts for movement in a particular direction.

But of course even the beginning painter experiences the push and pull of numerous vectors as he works, but no stylistic results. How does his situation, in which he has not found a way, differ from that of the artist who has?

Through years of work the artist finds that *in experience* certain of his wants take priority over, they seem more urgent than, others. And so too does certain color usage, thematic material, etc., seem not merely good but obligatory in their rightness. They conscript him. But beyond the obvious what this means is that the forces in the creative situation, which for the neophyte are a mass of tangled seethings and choice possibilities have in the artist moved closer to becoming System, in the sense in which our blood circulatory apparatus is System. Though there remain cross-currents and complexity, parts have become articulated, interconnected, cooperative, and the vital and the marginal have become relegated to their respective proper places. Necessity replaces choice. The artist "finds himself" by finding in the test of action, among things within and without himself, what is necessary and integral to him; he finds his calling by finding his callers. This is aesthetic growing up. And without this, one is ensnared in the tangle of one's amorphous yearnings and flitting choices and is not free. This ensnarement is the student's situation and in this respect it differs from the artist's. True, growing up may be a prelude to growing old, a hardening of the arteries of one's system, an inability to accommodate new forces when they intrude upon one's life. Artists recognize that styles may become ruts or graves if they do not stand open to new forces and confront their situations afresh each day, without presumption of the resultant. Yet despite the danger, style development is to be welcomed, as a requisite of freedom and as maturation.

It may now be clearer why I have claimed that schools cannot grant freedom but may strive to enable it; for freedom is dependent upon the developments cited, and these must be achieved, not simply licensed. I hope too that I have indicated *how* these strands of development are conducive to, and demanded by, such enablement.

And it seems to me that the educator who shapes his practices to enable freedom exhibits better reasons for what he does than one who, say, fosters skills just to be conservative, or fosters psychological growth because he is a tender-hearted (and tender-minded) therapist. The aims outlined are to help students *become painters* and if these aims include concern with more than just the craft of "painting," the goals are, because of their greater scope, not less but more professional; and if respect is to obtain among teachers and students, good reasons for what is done must be evident.

EDUCATIVE RESPONSIBILITY

Is fostering development along all these lines a responsibility of art teachers?

Irrespective of one's ethic, the responsibility for the developments cited will not be the teacher's alone, or even primarily his. No one is as responsible for the growth, welfare, and destiny of the painting student as is the student himself. And clearly when the teacher of painting is an artist, as he should be, neither his students nor his institution may ask that he give all of himself to teaching; the artist's rights as a man and even his teaching itself would suffer if such were asked. So the teacher will not assume unlimited or sole responsibility. Still, teaching requires competency, conscientiousness, caring; when students ask of their instructor bread he must not give them a stone out of clumsiness or indifference. The rub is that for some of the aforementioned growth strands—e.g., that of skillfulness—teachers have traditionally shown competency and shouldered a large measure of responsibility, but they have shown little aptitude or concern for fostering attitudinal and psychological maturation. Yet to the extent that the teacher brings little skill to and refuses responsibility for fostering maturation he withdraws from an educational task that, as just indicated, somehow, somewhere, and by someone needs doing. A teacher's refusal may be based upon the judgment that somewhere, someone other than himself should prompt such maturation and in some cases he will be right, but the burden remains imperative and hence his judgment should be reached with care, and, one hopes, with generosity.

However, there is a major barrier to the assumption of the responsibilities noted here. No teacher will shoulder burdens he thinks foolish for anyone to assume, and it is usually considered foolish to try to foster artistic maturation, as also to try to "teach creativity." However, by defining as we have the learnings artists achieve, we shake the notion that "maturity" and "creativity" are monolithic qualities, ones a teacher may or may not inject into a person lacking them. Rather, these terms are honorific, generic labels for people who understand their field, stand openly, grasp relationships, move with their feelings, have skills, etc.; thus the development of such particular capacities begins to seem possible.

And this development seems even more possible if a dynamic rather than static view of the learner is held, and if one's notion of what "teaching" means is also a broad and dynamic one.

Specifically, art teachers meet art students when the latter are not inert blocks but persons running the course of their lives. They are driven by hungers, lured on by aspirations, clouded by fears, pushed this way and that by obligations, desires, and demands. In practice they may sprint, trip, crawl, become immobilized, or recurrently reverse direction. But they are live creatures, moving, thrashing about, stalemated or whatever; a dynamic interplay of forces goes on in and about them. And now (to strain the metaphor) jogging up alongside such a student comes his art instructor, also running the course of his life, and with the situation so seen, i.e., dynamically, it seems to beg us to inquire as to what the meeting is to be (a parallel run? a brief bumping encounter? etc.), and what the run of the course is to do for the student (increase his skills? salve his psyche?) etc. That is, what is teachable and what teaching may be, are questions expanded in range as one sees the student not as clay acted upon by instructors but in the dynamic, interpersonal way cited.

For example, for the student lunging into art full speed ahead, "teaching" may mean giving him room to run, and, as a coach, checking his form, recommending diet, picking him up when he trips, helping him find equipment. And when the student who heretofore has seemed inert is seen dynamically instead, as immobilized by equal and contrary forces, which are, still, active within him, teaching may consist of bolstering some of these forces, defeating others, so that his system, no longer stalemated, moves again. For the apparently unimaginative student "teaching" may mean showing how art can be the shape of his hungers, the repository of his reveries, the surrogates for his otherwise unmanageable world; that is, a channeling into art of the dynamics of his inner life. And a student can be "taught" a great deal by the teacher's mere act of living as an artist and instructor, by his pursuing his way authentically and well, by his "going on," whether in peace or pain, by perseverance—something anyone who paints has to learn. That is, as always, the teacher teaches by being, among other things, a model. Sometimes he thusly teaches a posture or other thing essential but intangible. And sometimes he teaches even artistic methods via his model role, by exhibiting the manner in which he thinks and solves problems.

What then does teaching creativity mean? It is not

transforming one sort of creature into another or placing
abilities as by surgery into heads; it is meeting a dynamic
creature, the neophyte painter, and informing, freeing,
and coaching him, as student and instructor run together.
And the burden of doing such teaching, while not light, is
a bearable one. And the means of such teaching: demonstrations, counselling, role-playing, etc., have been natural
to, or learned by, many art instructors, and are ascertain-
able by others if they assume the responsibility of wanting
and finding them.

WHERE TO TEACH PAINTING

The art learnings cited have occurred through the ages
in numerous sorts of circumstances: apprenticeship systems, individual instruction by tutors, self-instruction, art
academies, college art programs. And since every age has
had its artists, it would be foolish to say that art learning
and teaching requires just this or that setting. Also, it
would be foolish to say that any specific setting or method
one names *assures* the learnings cited. However, it is never
foolish to ask about how the currently prevalent way of
educating artists can be improved. And if this way is
troubled, as is the case, such inquiry seems inescapable.

Today, ever greater proportions of our neophyte artists
are coming to college and university campuses for their
education, both general and artistic. The liberalization of
their intellects and the stimulation of ideas thus afforded
are valuable enough to assure continuance of university
attendance by young artists, aside from the degrees
granted being practically useful. But to pay for these values
with a thwarting art program seems horribly compromis-
ing to young painters. Since they will not move elsewhere,

what can be done to improve the college setting for art programs?

Consider the current situation. Students are placed for art study in regularized courses, a practice which fits them into the scholastic framework but runs counter to the way art abilities are achieved and art created, in that working in the posture of the artist entails openness, and practice in this posture is necessary for learning; and how can one stand openly in the grip of a time schedule? Also, grades are given, yet evaluation is so highly personal, often influenced by one's spiritual kinship to the artist, as to be untrustworthy as an objective measurement of worth. And evaluating precisely at semester's end seems meaningless; to work, show, and get responses to one's work is an inevitable pattern in the painter's life, but why in December and June necessarily? And with less and less contact between teacher and student characterizing our changing university campuses, how is the intimate coaching I cited to obtain?

A simple expedient would greatly improve the possibilities for art educational practices on campuses and yet be economically and otherwise practicable. The university now grants to its art department the right to judge its students' competence in art. And this is an act of faith, inevitable because few deans and presidents know enough to act as judges in this matter. But now the faith is exercized on regular occasions and placed piecemeal. For example, the administration says: "Six points are to be recorded for student Brown when Professor Smith (we have faith in him) in December says 'Brown passed Life Drawing I,' and another six when Professor Jones (we have faith in him, too) in June says, 'Brown passed Oil Painting.'" Yet without sacrificing anyone's prerogatives, time, effort, or money, the university could say to its art department and art students, "Take this time the student spends here in art classes and art practice, this half (or whatever fraction) of his university life. You are responsible for it and judge it, any way. But hereafter, do not feel obliged to fix courses, class hours, grades, credits. Organize it as you will, to best foster the goals you are, anyway, seeking. Student Brown, we will give you sixty points, half the number for your degree, when the department assures the administration that you've met their standards of effort and achievement and hence that the college is safe in certifying you as a graduate."

There seems, apathy and bookkeeping considerations aside, no reason for refusing this suggestion. And its possibilities of opening up the program and of better curricula planning approaches seem to endorse the suggestion strongly. For example, students' work patterns could be individually and uniquely established in accordance with individual abilities, goals, and needs, and altered as and when necessary. The pattern need not be programs of courses. The key activity might be a Tutorial Seminar, with an experienced professor-coach, to stimulate, guide, advise students, to share in shaping their work and study plans. Such work and study would occur sometimes singly, and sometimes, as when numerous individuals have needs in common, in groups under younger instructors. The aim of planning would be to meet the individual's lacks, expand his strengths, foster growth *as* and *when* needed along the strands of growth cited; this would allow learning to be a response to a need made evident. A poor draftsman might spend half his art-time drawing, but being, say, a brilliant colorist, he might never take, as he would have to otherwise, a prescribed year of Color and Design. The student hungering to paint would not need to fulfill prerequisites before painting—his hunger could otherwise expire for lack of gratification—the skills he needs could be sought, when upon *painting*, the student under advisement sees he needs them.

Also, in this scheme, the art of painting would not be, implicitly, fragmented into Drawing, Designing, and Painting (proper), a fragmentation occurring now through our colleges' insistence that everyone take separate courses so labelled and hence implying their difference each from the others. It is not painting which demands this fragmentation, for every time a dab of paint is applied it is of course *painting*, but in that it delineates or defines it also functions as *drawing*, and in that it is part of a total organized contrivance, it also functions as *design;* and it is all these at once. Of course, isolation of, say, color problems, from all others makes these more manageable, and to this end a student (or several) whose paintings are poor in color may be told to study color outside of, and in addition to, paintings-as-such—perhaps under instruction. *Such* isolation, when and as needed, only implies special attention to a facet of a still unitary act. But programming courses in design and drawing for all, irrespective of, and prior to, discernment of individual needs, is demanded only by scholastic requirements; it makes possible grade-giving in small pieces and it facilitates the processing of numerous students toward skillfulness. It alleviates the educator's need to examine individuals, but in so doing it lies about the unity of painting and reduces the meaningfulness of the learning process. And if, as I am suggesting, paintings are brought back to the seminar for discussion, and new ideas and further plans are continuingly made, based upon the current status of the art student and goals of teacher and student, then such preordained processing becomes unnecessary as well as unwise. The student's achievement of fundamental and other skills can be insisted upon as strongly by one's mentor and in a seminar as in an impersonal college catalogue, and more cogently since the need for doing so can be made clear.

I am urging not an unstructured or tender situation for art students. Teachers may be directive or not, as they think beneficial for each of their students. And a display of the instructor's biases, even were it not inevitable, is often a helpful challenge to students and prompts examination of views. The mentor is not to be a father, saint, or psychiatrist. And if some sorts of study are best routinized then so they should be. I am only urging that the characteristics of art, and how men develop as artists, be the chief determinants of art teaching and programs, that programs be structured as and when and how these characteristics demand, that actual practice may be tougher than is currently common *or* more tender as cases vary and as needs arise, but that such cases and needs and not scholastic habits shape the education of painters.

Finally, another sort of aid to the development of painters can be afforded in the setting I suggest better than in most current situations.

Instruction, of course, cannot prepare the artist for the task of coping in and with his personal inner life in art, but a preview of the problems involved, and discussion of the bases of them and how one may manage oneself so as to stay afloat with them could be helpful. For example, young artists often do not know how to take the criticism they receive upon exhibiting their work. Taking it as the objective truth about their painting, they can be inflated or shattered; refusing to take it at all may protect the ego but may induce blindness to actual assets or shortcomings. And how is one to live with the feelings induced by the way one takes criticism? On what may one's self-respect rest? How to cohere, to stay firm? Another problem: every reputable person who has written on art has described its function in life in terms of services to the artist's or community's life, or to God or the State, with the artist fulfilling what he understands to be his part in this functioning. Yet, while art is invariably still so described, a Hollywood-like star system prevails on the art scene, not with service to oneself, community, God, or State as the measure of artists, but box-office attraction and newsworthiness. How does one maintain the inner strength to go on his own quest, without excessive awareness of the crowd which would praise or abuse him according to the business, news, or entertainment value of this quest? How does he maintain autonomy? And, how can one remain an artist even if he fears he will never become a matinee idol, or if, upon reaching forty and having made all the headlines, he has ceased to be newsworthy and is then forgotten? If one works out of personal necessity or his sense of a calling, then fulfilling those needs his art can fulfill will sustain him, whether he is applauded or not. But artists are often torn between the feeling that they are great and the contrary feeling that they are worthless, and to live without external confirmation of the former leaves them shaky. Probably more souls are sold for such confirmation than for money. Recognition in the schools of the occurrence of such problems, and of their sources, could be valuable. Most important would be recognition of the feeling-states in the artist's life, of disappointment, elation, the disorientations of failure and success, and of how one may live with them. Such preparation for not only painting but being a painter, though doomed to be less than fully adequate, would still be useful and welcomed. And in the scheme of organization I sketched this could be readily undertaken, while difficult in more rigid, impersonal, segmented structures.

THE STANCE OF THE ARTIST

Finally, a suggestion for education in art outside of professional art training. This education should, of course, be a matter of concern to artists who care about the welfare of their field, because in art as elsewhere one's professional education rests (or founders) upon one's early learnings and preparation for growth. Also, art will be for the populace largely what art education makes of it for them in non-professional schooling, and hence the quality of the art public rests upon art education's efforts.

My suggestion is that all art education be conducted as though each student, youngster or adult, were going to become a professional artist, particularly to the effect that each person be encouraged and helped to work in the posture and with the values and aims of the artist.

Now I know that to many art educators this suggestion will seem unfortunate on the face of it, for they will recall the stultifying effects upon children of academic art training made child-size for the schools. As it was once current, such training meant learning perspective, rendering, anatomy, etc., irrespective of children's drives and development levels. Hence it was educationally irrelevent and unfeasible, and it robbed childhood of its childlikeness. Moreover, ironically, it robbed art of all that art is most valued for, and there is the point. If the foregoing pages make sense then it should be clear that "working in the posture of the artist" entails no personally meaningless exercises. The mistake previously made was that the child was made to stand like an academic adult, attempting to achieve the skills prescribed by the academy; we have come to see that the genuine adult artist, though his career entails study and labor, stands much like a child (the innocent in a world as yet unmade). And to ask the child to work in the artist's posture entails, insofar as childhood's natural propensity is concerned, no hardship. It entails, to repeat, openness, responsiveness to intuition and feeling, seeing afresh, a materialization of one's amorphous loves. It would seem that the child and the teacher who cares about him cannot object to a stance so characterized.

But my suggestion is to some practical point; it is not so unobjectionable as to be already agreed upon and implemented by art educators. For working in the stance of the artist also entails the positing that art *matters,* and that *adequacy* of expression, not merely expressive efforts, is indispensable, and that one's artistic abilities and sensitivities ought to be conscientiously developed, and that one's way is *to be followed;* it is obligatory. Which is to say that such a posture is antithetical to that art teaching, quite current, practiced as "playing around with art materials," or as a *means,* say, to the liberally educated mind, or to the child's emotional and mental development, or to community improvement. In advocating the stance of the artist for all art classes I am, then, confronting a real opposition.

My reasons for so doing are several. First, it would seem that those children who are eventually to become artists deserve some preparation for their profession prior to art school or college. Such preparation is, after all, afforded persons in every other field. It is true, of course, that these children usually cannot be identified early, and in any case the artistically gifted are a small minority, but art *is* taught, and if taught surely prospective artists should not be penalized by the omissions and commissions of this teaching. They should not be steeped in attitudes which they must eventually shed—not by people who purport to value art. They must not, that is, be told to hold art as a *means* when artists hold art to be an end, or told to regard novel use of art materials, or pretty patterning, as identical with pursuit of artistic necessitation and aesthetic development. They can only be hindered by such attitudes.

Yet my suggestion is not to hurt the majority for the sake of the artistic minority. On the contrary. I know art educators will object that, however important art is to artists, educators cannot seriously maintain that to them and most of their students, the achievement of, say, aesthetic excellence ought to loom as more important than intellectual and emotional maturation. But one ought to see that *whatever* one's educational goals, when art serves them at all it serves by standing as a master and not a servant. Self-interest is not always best served by one being interested in oneself but sometimes by denying such interest and giving oneself to a glowing Cause. The giving happily boomerangs into a getting. And with art one gets what it has to give by adopting its stance. Much as one does not learn what science is all about by mere handling of test tubes, formulas, and scales but rather by acquiring the scientist's objective stance, his habitual skepticism, his ways of organizing data into schema, in short in becoming intimate with his way of standing in the world, so one learns what art is, not through doing art-like motions with art materials but through standing as the artist does. For art's contribution to *general* education such standing is necessary, and not for professional training alone. Through such standing one comes to know what art is at base all about. By looking to the artist's star, one gains whatever emotional development art affords. The majority of educators and of children will, then, be helped and not hurt by art education practiced in the posture of the professional artist.

And this would have the additional effect of fostering a greater feeling of community between artists and art teachers at all levels: a feeling rather rare these days. A difference of personality type between teacher and artist accounts for some of their distance from each other; the man who volunteers for the local civil service is often quite different from one who volunteers for bohemia. Yet this gap is only a sometime thing. The bigger gap is between people who take art as paramount and a way of life and those who apparently treat it as mere fun or decoration or a means to an end. When this gap exists— and it is decreasing—we cannot find a kinship between art professionals and teachers. In the sciences, we know, efforts have been made to have professional physicists help with the design of elementary science programs; fostering the capacity to think scientifically is, we insist, a concern transcending school limits and levels. A parallel in art can occur, but only if artists find a community of aims and attitudes among themselves and those who teach art. And such community is not precluded by educator's objectives; indeed such objectives call for the posture which would foster this community, the stance of the artist.

Notes

CHAPTER 1: THE ART-APPRECIATIVE PHENOMENON AND ITS OBJECT

1. This quality of appreciative experience is pointed out by Professor Albert Hofstater in his lectures in aesthetics at Columbia University.
2. The line of thinking here stems—and deviates—from Edmund Husserl's *Ideas: General Introduction to Pure Phenomenology*, translated by W. R. B. Gibson (London: George Allen and Unwin Ltd.), 1931.
3. Kant stated a closely related idea: "In a product of beautiful Art, we must become conscious that it is art and not nature; but yet the purposiveness in its form must seem to be as free from constraint of arbitrary rules as if it were a product of mere nature." Immanuel Kant, *Critique of Judgment*, tr. J. H. Bernard (New York: Hafner Publishing Co., 1951) p. 249.
4. Etienne Gilson refers to works of art as individuals and for this means of conveying the idea, though not for the following amplification of it, I am indebted to him. See Etienne Gilson, *Painting and Reality* (New York: Meridian Books, Inc.), 1959.
5. Lincoln Rothschild, *Style in Art* (New York: Thomas Yoseloff, 1960).
6. Freud's allegation that this effect explains the gratification af-

forded by some poetry and novels might, one guesses, be extended by him to fit the cited sort of painting—though extendable to few others.

7. Karl Jaspers, *Truth and Symbol*. Trans. by J. T. Wilder, W. Kluback, W. Kimmel (New York: Twayne Publishers, 1959).
8. See Morris Weitz' article in his anthology, *Problems in Aesthetics* (New York: Macmillan Co., 1959).
9. Morris Philipson says aestheticians are no longer even attempting such ventures. See the introduction to his *Aesthetics Today* (New York: World Publishing Co., 1961).

CHAPTER 2: THE ARTIST AT WORK

1. Brewster Ghiselin, *The Creative Process* (New York: New American Library, 1955), p. 15.
2. James L. Jarrett, *The Quest for Beauty* (New York: Prentice-Hall, Inc., 1957), p. 96.

CHAPTER 3: ART AND AUDIENCE

1. Alan W. Watts, *Psychotherapy, East and West* (New York: New American Library, 1963).

Bibliography

Work used in preparation of this volume and of interest to the student.

BOOKS

ARISTOTLE. *On Poetry and Music*. Translated by S. H. Butcher. New York: Liberal Arts Press, 1926.

ARNHEIM, RUDOLPH. *Art and Visual Perception*. Berkeley, California: University of California Press, 1954.

BELL, CLIVE. *Art*. London: Chatto and Windus, Ltd., 1914.

BENOIT, HUBERT. *The Supreme Doctrine*. New York: Viking Press, 1959.

COLLINGWOOD, R. G. *The Principles of Art*. Oxford: Clarendon Press, 1938.

CONANT, JAMES B. *Modern Science and Modern Man.* New York: Doubleday and Co., Inc., 1952.

CROCE, BENEDETTO. *The Essence of Aesthetic.* Translated by Douglas Ainslee. London: William Heinemann, 1921.

DEWEY, JOHN. *Art as Experience.* New York: Minton Balch and Co., 1934.

EDMAN, IRWIN. *Arts and the Man.* New York: New American Library, 1949.

FREUD, SIGMUND. *Leonardo da Vinci: A Study in Psycho-Sexuality.* Translated by A. A. Brill. New York: Random House, 1947.

FROMM, ERICH. *The Art of Loving.* New York: Harper and Bros., 1956.

FRY, ROGER. *Vision and Design.* London: Chatto and Windus, Ltd., 1925.

GHISELIN, BREWSTER. *The Creative Process.* New York: New American Library, 1955.

GILBERT, KATHERINE E. and KUHN, HELMUT. *A History of Aesthetics.* Bloomington, Indiana: Indiana University Press, 1954.

GILSON, ETIENNE. *Painting and Reality.* New York: Meridian Books, Inc., 1959.

GOLDWATER, ROBERT. *Artists on Art.* New York: Pantheon Books, Inc., 1945.

HUSSERL, EDMUND. *Ideas: General Introduction to Pure Phenomenology.* Translated by W. R. B. Gibson. London: George Allen and Unwin, Ltd., 1931.

JARRETT, JAMES L. *The Quest for Beauty.* New York: Prentice-Hall, Inc., 1957.

JASPERS, KARL. *Truth and Symbol*. Translated by J. T. Wilde, W. Kluback, W. Kimmel, Twayne Publishers, New York, 1959.

JUNG, KARL. *Modern Man in Search of a Soul*. London: K. Paul, Trench & Trobner & Co., Ltd., 1933.

————. *Psyche and Symbol*. Edited by Violet S. de Laszlo. New York: Doubleday and Co., 1959.

KANT, IMMANUEL. *Critique of Judgment*. Translated by J. H. Bernard. New York: Hafner Publishing Co., 1951.

KAUFMANN, WALTER. ed. *Existentialism from Dostoievsky to Sartre*. New York: Meridian Books, Inc., 1956.

KITTO, H. D. E. *The Greeks*. Harmondsworth, Middlesex: Penguin Books, Ltd.

LANGER, SUZANNE K. *Problems of Art*. New York: Charles Scribners Sons, 1957.

————. *Philosophy in a New Key*. New York: New American Library, 1948.

MACHOVER, KAREN. *Personality Projection in the Drawing of the Human Figure*. Springfield, Illinois: C. C. Thomas, 1949.

MARITAIN, JACQUES. *The Responsibility of the Artist*. New York: Charles Scribners Sons, 1960.

MUMFORD, LEWIS. *Art and Technics*. New York: Columbia University Press, 1952.

PANOFSKY, ERWIN. *Meaning in the Visual Arts*. New York: Doubleday and Co., Inc., 1957.

PELLES, GERALDINE. *Art, Artists and Society*. Englewood Cliffs, New Jersey: Prentice-Hall, Inc., 1965.

PHILIPSON, MORRIS. *Aesthetics Today*. New York: World Publishing Co., 1961.

PLATO. *Symposium*. Translated by John C. G. Rouse. New York: New American Library, 1956.

PLOTINUS. *The Enneads.* Translated by Stephen McKenna. London: Faber and Faber, Ltd., 1930.

RANK, OTTO. *Arts and Artists.* New York: Alfred Knopf and Co., 1932.

ROSENBERG, HAROLD. *The Tradition of the New.* New York: Horizon Press, 1959.

ROTHSCHILD, LINCOLN. *Style in Art.* New York and London: Thomas Yoseloff, 1960.

SANTAYANA, GEORGE. *The Sense of Beauty.* Dover Publications Inc., 1955.

SCHILP, PAUL A. (Editor). *The Philosophy of Karl Jaspers.* New York: Tudor Publishing Co., 1957.

SHAHN, BEN. *The Shape of Content.* New York: Vintage Books, 1960.

SUZUKI, D. T. *Zen Buddhism.* Edited by Wm. Barrett. New York: Doubleday and Co., Inc., 1956.

ST. AUGUSTINE. *On Christian Doctrine.* Translated by D. W. Robertson, Jr. The Liberal Arts Press, 1958.

VIVAS, ELISEO and KRIEGER, MURRAY, editors. *The Problems of Aesthetics.* New York: Rinehart and Co., Inc., 1953.

WATTS, ALAN W. *The Way of Zen.* New York: New American Library, 1957.

———. *Psychotherapy, East and West,* New York: New American Library, 1963.

WEITZ, MORRIS, editor. *Problems in Aesthetics.* New York: Macmillan Co., 1959.

WHITE, MORTON, editor. *The Age of Analysis.* New York: New American Library, 1955.

ARTICLES

BULLOUGH, EDWARD. "Psychical Distance as a Factor in Art and an Aesthetic Principle," *British Journal of Psychology,* V, 1912.

SCHAPIRO, MEYER. "Leonardo and Freud: An Art Historical Study," *Journal of the History of Ideas* (April, 1956).

Index

DATE DUE

JAO 3'88			

DEMCO 25-380